Kend Philpott

Patti L. Philpott

If the Devil
Wrote a Bible

by **Kent Allan Philpott** and **Katie L. C. Philpott**

EVP

Earthen Vessel Publishing
San Rafael, California

If the Devil Wrote a Bible

Published 2013 by
Earthen Vessel Publishing
San Rafael, CA 94903
www.evpbooks.com

Interior Book Design and Layout by
Katie L. C. Philpott
Cover Design by Michelle Shelfer

Editing by Tom Jerrells and Michelle Shelfer

ISBN: 978-0-9703296-7-7 (print version)
ISBN: 978-0-9703296-9-1 (ebook version)

Contents

Preface

In 1974 Logos International published the first edition of *If the Devil Wrote a Bible*. It did quite well and then Logos International closed down, but the book has apparently kept right on. Recently, a friend pointed out that Amazon.com carried a pirated form of the book published by someone or another and that it was selling briskly. I found an old copy in my office and realized that the book needed updating and that new material could be added. Therefore, in order to keep up with the times, a new edition of the Devil's bible is presented here.

The Chief Demon delivers nothing actually new; he simply spins old ideas for a new generation in order to ensnare new followers. And he keeps getting new disciples. Deception never stops; his lies get bigger and bigger. It seems that the wilder the whopper the more quickly people rush to embrace it.

No, the Devil has not written an actual bible, but he has spoken and written through others over the millennia, to the point that the Prince of Demons might as well have a bible of his own.

This is not *Screwtape Letters*, and I am not C.S. Lewis. That book was and is a favorite of mine, and over the years I have given away many copies of it as part of my pastoral ministry. Just as Lewis, I do take the Devil seriously. There is a Devil, of that I am certain.

Katie and I use a special name for God: "YouKnowWho," abbreviated to "YKW." Satan, we imagine, would shy away from using a real biblical name for the Creator of the universe. We think that the Devil hates the name of God and would intentionally avoid using it at all costs. Please do not take offense at us here; we are simply keeping in literary character.

There are three main parts to this book. One is the new chapter material; the other two parts, which we thought would be essential to fully describe the thoughts and intentions of the Devil are the "Demonments" and the "Bebaditudes."

We have no illusion that we have captured the thoughts of the Devil in this book. The material is based upon our understanding of Scripture and upon our experience in dealing with the Devil. During my five years as a street preacher in San Francisco's Haight-Ashbury District, I learned something about the tricks of the Devil in occult and eastern religious practices and saw the impact on the mind and emotions of drugs like LSD, peyote, mescaline, psilocybin, and marijuana. Then followed decades of pastoral ministry, all in the San Francisco Bay Area, and thirty years as a volunteer at San Quentin Prison. While at Golden Gate Theological Seminary in Mill Valley, California, I wrote *A Manual of Demonology and the Occult*, which was later published by Zondervan Publishing House. After that I wrote two more books dealing with a similar theme, the newest of which is *How Christians Cast out Demons Today* (Earthen Vessel Publishing, 2011).

We may be wrong, but the Devil's bible, his written means of trapping and deceiving, has become more sophisticated and nuanced than it was even forty-plus years ago when the first edition was published.

The Devil is not lazy or stupid. Rather, the evidence reveals that the Devil adapts to the times and probably even influences culture in ways we will neither see nor understand.

Satan does not want to lose even one poor little sheep to his Enemy and so rises to meet the needs of each generation. However, whatever strategies and tactics Satan tries, God is constantly working to claim His own, and He will not be thwarted.

Christians do not hold a dualistic philosophy; that is, we do not adhere to a worldview wherein there is a war of gods, one evil and one good, fighting it out on a cosmic scale. Far from it. What we find in Scripture is that the Creator God is Sovereign Lord of all, but there is present in the universe an evil being, a fallen angel at the head of a host of fallen angels, otherwise known as demons.[1] This Satan – a being who wars against God, for that is the meaning of the name Satan – has certain but limited powers. There are gaps in the revealed Scripture in regard to details about the Devil, and we are thus tempted to fill in those gaps, but to do so would go beyond Scripture itself. And this we want to avoid.

However powerful Satan may be or appear to be, still the enemy of God is defeated and under the authority of Him whom even the Devil and his demons recognize is the Lord God Almighty. There is no battle of equals, but there is nevertheless spiritual warfare that goes on, which is the reason for the second advent of *If the Devil Wrote a Bible*.

---

1   For a further discussion on demons see our book *How Christians Cast Out Demons Today*. It may be ordered at www.evpbooks.com.

The Devil's Introduction

Dear Reader, you've been duped. You are the victim of a deliberate and systematic brainwashing effort perpetrated by a tyrant whose sole desire is to take all pleasure and freedom out of your life and cause you to submit to his overarching system of rules and regulations. He commissioned a detestable book, the so-called Holy Bible, a best-seller for generations, found in every hotel room from San Francisco to Schenectady, as well as on the shelves of most homes, gathering dust and taking up space. You'd think that if it were such a successful work it must be an excellent text and have some wisdom to offer. The truth is, no one could possibly read it all the way through, because it's like wading through mud. Its success is derived solely from the human need to feel like a "good person" and point to it on the bookshelf.

Although I am clearly the main attraction in that other book, my story is told therein by my enemy. Is that fair? The object of this endeavor is the long overdue correction of a terrible wrong perpetrated on Me and on the truth by my adversary. I consider it my duty to correct the misconceptions promoted by him by means of his insufferable tome, *his* bible.

I refuse to use my enemy's name because it is abhorrent to Me. I refer to him as You Know Who, or YKW for short. He makes himself out to be some sort of god, but what about Me? My enemy calls himself the great I AM, but I am the

Great I AM ME, and I have been here almost from the beginning, unlike the humans YKW used to write his bible, as if he couldn't do it himself. He really scraped the bottom of the dung barrel to expect such a collection of criminals and low-lifers to represent his "high mightiness." Utter foolishness, in my judgment.

Take Moses, a pampered palace kid who murdered when things didn't go his way, then ran away for forty years, cowering in the desert. Then there's Joshua, an obsessed warmonger yet an obvious coward, judging by how often YKW had to tell him to "take courage" and "don't be afraid."[1] And there's all the pathetic, so-called "judges," who didn't deserve space on a scroll. And Samuel, who couldn't even control his own sons from corruption. And David, who was the biggest fraud of that older collection of confusing books they call the "Old Testament." He somehow got a reputation for being a daddy's boy – "a man after YKW's own heart"[2] – when he was really a vicious saber-rattler ("struck down his ten thousands"[3]), a terrible parent, an adulterer, and a murderer. Next came his son Solomon, claiming great wisdom, who just kissed up to YKW by building that huge, garish temple, hoping YKW would turn a blind eye to his shenanigans with hundreds of foreign women and their gods. Then there's a rag-tag bunch of pathetic prophets who whined continually about Israel's sin in leaving YKW for other (better) gods.

As if that weren't bad enough, there is a "New Testament" (because YKW's ghost writers obviously didn't get it right the first time). Take Matthew, who was a hated tax collector and betrayer of his people; or John, who should have been certified as a lunatic, considering that fantastical "Revelation" hallucination; or Luke, who fancied himself a historian, when he should have stuck to practicing medicine (maybe he wasn't

---

1   See Joshua 1:6, 9, 18

2   See 1 Samuel 13:14

3   See 1 Samuel 18:7

good enough to keep a patient clientele). The biggest misfit of all was Paul, who was a murderer several times over and even admitted to being the "foremost of sinners"[4] and not good enough to be more than a slave.[5] He washed out on his noble mission of keeping those earliest Christians in check, then pretended to be accosted and struck blind by the very god he then touted as lord and savior. From great rabbi to executed criminal – what a waste!

I, the Great I AM ME, do not rely on others to do what I am competent to do, which is to tell *my* story, *my* way, so I have written *my* own book. Words, ideas, philosophies, imaginings, dreams, and visions are all packaged just right. *My* Bible, filled with *my* wisdom and *my* sayings. *My* testament is more relevant than my enemy's book. I have constructed clever axioms connected brilliantly to appeal to mind and body and are just shades away from the so-called "truth." Attractive, alluring, and sexy, my wisdom is packaged into catchy sayings and concepts, sculpted to fit into any current culture. I am the cool philosopher, the guru, the spiritual master, and the religious leader. I am quite adept at using humanity's own art, music, science, and literature, embedding in them *my* truth. *My* kind of truth is bound to make them skeptical, even contemptuous of YKW. Yes, I will prevail, and many will be convinced.

So, I have finally put right what YKW distorted after he unfairly threw Me out of my own home because he didn't approve of Me. He would have you think I am "rebellious," that I made my move and lost, but I have a better agenda. Yes, I may have to resort to stealing, killing, and lying, but only because I want you to enjoy my presence for all eternity. You see, I have a special place I've prepared just for you, and I will escort you there myself. I also have my own army of angels and helpers to guide you along the way until you can

---

4   See 1 Timothy 1:15

5   See Romans 1:1; Galatians 1:10

rest in the warmth of your eternal abode. Until then, Dear Reader, take this most valuable Devil's Bible, read, consider, and follow every word I have written.

Now then, here is my masterpiece.

Signed:

Lucifer, also known as the Devil or Satan, Chief Adversary of YKW.

• •

Publisher's note:

The Devil has indeed written a bible, one suited for modern generations. He submitted the manuscript for publication, assuming it would be printed as-is. Unfortunately for him, that was not to be.

A certain unnamed Christian was asked to provide commentary on what the Devil has written. Do not be surprised when you see, right inside these pages, critical replies to the Devil's declarations and claims under the headings titled "A Christian's Response." Here is that Christian's personal explanation for the way the task was approached:

> Why was I chosen to be the one to provide a Christian response to the Devil's bible? I don't really know why. I only know that I have been pastoring a small Baptist church in northern California for the last twenty-nine years, and regarding the Devil and his bag of tricks, I have seen it all. I was privileged to be part of a movement of God that took place all around me in the late 60's and early 70's, sometimes called the Jesus People Movement. During that time an unprecedented number of people were filled with a hunger to know the One True God and a willingness to invite Him into their lives. It was a marvelous time, but I found that wherever God moved, the Devil

soon followed. It became necessary for me at that time to come to the aid of some of those who wished to be freed from the Devil's clutches. I saw him move in startling and supernatural ways, from common garden-variety demonic possession to dramatic, unholy "signs and wonders." I was able to help people to get free and to come to understand the nature of evil, repentance, and the grace of God and His[6] mercy.

In addition, a master's thesis entitled *A Manual of Demonology and the Occult*, published by Zondervan Publishing House in 1973, gave me the opportunity to do research on that subject over a period of three years.

I guess you could say I know the Devil's tricks pretty well, and they don't scare me. I stand firmly on the Truth of the Bible and need no further armor than the Word of God to protect me.

Finally, a chief reason I agreed to this project is that a mere exposure to the Devil's thinking is of value, because simply knowing how Satan operates should be sufficient warning. However, since the Devil does "blind the minds," a Christian's commentary makes sense.

---

6   While quotations from the ESV Bible do not capitalize "He," "His," and "Him" in reference to members of the Holy Trinity, we will follow this convention within "A Christian's Response" sections.

In the Beginning...

I was there; I overheard the conversation. I knew what was afoot and I wanted a part in it, a big part.

In the beginning, indeed; the grand stage was set, but I was given the role of antagonist and shuttled off to a mere subplot. Why I wasn't forever banished to outer darkness I do not know, but here I am still, and I will do my best to frustrate the writer of the script.

Act 1, scene 1 - a garden called Eden. I will be a snake hiding in the grass, and I will strike before anyone notices. I'll steal the show.

Chapter 1:
How I Stole the Show

The serpent said to the lady: "You will not surely die. For YKW knows that when you eat of it your eyes will be opened, and you will be like him, knowing good and evil."

The Devil's Commentary

Note that some of my most quotable sayings appear at the beginning of each chapter in my bible. And lest you, Dear Reader, do not quite understand my succinct declarative verses, I have added my own commentary as expansion and explanation.

"You will not surely die." This is the first thing I ever said directly to humans, but it certainly has not been the last.

What we have here is a story about two trees in a garden. YKW would have you think this place was some sort of paradise, but when the landlord requires strict obedience to arbitrary rules and regulations and enforces his law with the threat of death, what sort of paradise is that?

One tree was called the "Tree of the Knowledge of Good and Evil." The other tree was called the "Tree of Life." Adam and Eve were told by that tyrant not to eat from the Tree of the Knowledge of Good and Evil or they would die.

I thought it best to assure Eve that she would indeed *not* die if she took a bite. YKW told her she would die; I told her she would not die, and of course I was right. Eve hadn't been around long enough to know that she had to eat the fruit of the Tree of Life to live forever, and she didn't even understand the concept of dying. I saw no need to explain that to her or that her disobedience would mean removal from the garden and thus loss of access to the Tree of Life. I wanted her to die; you see I hated the woman and her man, because YKW made them in his image and loved them. I hate all humans. Of course that doesn't include you, Dear Reader – you're special.

Thus I opened up poor Eve's pathetic little mind to a greater understanding by telling her that by eating the fruit of the Tree of the Knowledge of Good and Evil she would become equal with YKW. And furthermore, I revealed that YKW did not want her to achieve such an exalted position and had actually hidden such a divine "truth" from her deliberately. You see, I believe in equality, while YKW prefers to rule by dictatorship.

By means of this simple reframing of the truth I was able to separate the humans from their creator, of course, for their own good. I saved them from a cruel overlord who only wants to take all the fun out of life with his unreasonable demands. I have since built on this victory with Eve to reinforce that what I have to offer as outlined in my Bible is far superior to the vague promises of that other bible.

• •

A Christian's response

The Devil[1] did, in fact, say to the woman known as Eve, "You will not surely die." This statement is actually in a Bible, but not the Devil's. It is found in Genesis, the first book of the Hebrew Scriptures, sometimes called the Old Testament:

Now the serpent was more crafty than any

---

1   Devil, *diabolos* in the Greek, from which the word "Devil" is derived, literally means "thrown-through." The idea is that the Devil divides, sets at variance, separates, creates factions, and so on. "Devil" will be capitalized to distinguish a title for a specific entity from "devil(s)" as a generic term.

other beast of the field that the LORD God had made. He said to the woman, "Did God actually say, 'You shall not eat of any tree in the garden'?" And the woman said to the serpent, "We may eat of the fruit of the trees in the garden, but God said, 'You shall not eat of the fruit of the tree that is in the midst of the garden, neither shall you touch it, lest you die.'" But the serpent said to the woman, "You will not surely die. For God knows that when you eat of it your eyes will be opened, and you will be like God, knowing good and evil."
Genesis 3:1-5[2]

Who is the serpent? Simply put, the serpent is the Devil himself, or maybe that should be "itself." The Devil is an *it*, neither male nor female.[3] The Devil may appear as either gender, however. When the Devil shows up as a male he is referred to as an incubus, and when it appears as a female she is a succubus. In Genesis, the Devil is a serpent and sneaky-smart.

The Devil is a great liar. He twisted words and lured the woman with the possibility of living forever and being like God. Nothing much has changed over the course of human history; we still want to know more and have more power than God gave us.

---

2   In the "Christian's Response" sections, several terms will be used for The Holy Bible: "Hebrew Scriptures," meaning the Old Testament as contrasted with the New Testament; "the Bible," meaning both the Old Testament and New Testament together; "God's Word," meaning any part of the Bible; "the real Bible," meaning the Bible; and "the Scriptures," meaning the Bible. The Old Testament was written in stages between c. 1450 B.C. and c. 450 B.C. The New Testament was written during the first century C.E.

3   The Greek New Testament does use the masculine personal pronoun to describe Satan and therefore "he" and "him" will be used to conform to standard biblical usage. But, Satan is still an "it."

If the Devil wrote a bible, really laid it out in published form, it might be hard to discern his deception. After all, Eve did not detect the lie. She must have thought she could get something for nothing, or maybe she thought she was being cheated by God by not having enough knowledge. To know what God knows was part of the enticement.

The Devil was in the form or body of a snake. Maybe that was a case of possession, or perhaps it was imitation. The Devil can look like anything. One never knows what-is-what with the Devil. One time he is obviously a fire-breathing demon complete with red suit and pitchfork, another time an angel, even an "angel of light."[4] A prophet once named the Devil "Lucifer," meaning Day Star or Morning Star.[5] He is crafty, super smart, beautiful, and deceptive, all the while being a liar, murderer, and rebel against God, bent on warfare against all that He has made.

Eve did not die. She ate from the tree and even became the first evangelist of sorts when she convinced her husband Adam to eat from it as well; but she did not die. The Devil was right. Or was he?

What happened? First of all, Eve's eyes were indeed opened, along with those of her husband. Right away they discovered they were naked. They had been naked all along, but it had not been an issue. Now they hid from one another, sewing fig leaves together to cover their genitals. Ever since, we have been paying the price in guilt and shame associated with our sexuality, and sexuality is right at the core of our being. The Devil spoke a lie, and there was a great Fall, and no human being has ever been able to repair the damage.

---

4   2 Corinthians 11:14: "And no wonder, for even Satan disguises himself as an angel of light."

5   Isaiah 14:12: "How you are fallen from heaven, O Day Star, son of Dawn! How you are cut down to the ground, you who laid the nations low!"

Next, Eve and Adam hid from God. When He came calling on the man and his wife in the garden, they hid because they were afraid. For the first time fear was a factor in their lives. Fear of being in God's presence had never previously existed; they had enjoyed a close and personal relationship with their Maker, but now God was to be feared. God called out, and Adam spoke up and confessed he was afraid because he was naked. That is what he said, because that is what he felt. Innocence was lost. Adam and Eve then compounded the tragedy by blaming. Eve blamed the serpent, and Adam blamed her. All fellowship, not only between Adam and Eve, but also between humans and God, was damaged severely. Where intimacy, freedom, and openness had been, now fear, shame, hiding, and blaming would characterize human existence. Attempts to recover that joy, knowledge of which might be written into our very being, has marked human religious history.

After the Fall, the lives of the first man and woman were altered dramatically. For the woman, there would be pain in childbirth, and there would be confusion and power struggles between a woman and her husband. The man would find life hard; he would no longer live in a garden full of easily obtained food. Now survival would mean hard work for the remainder of his life. Instead of fun in the sun in the garden with a beautiful wife, Adam would be separated from her as each sweated and fought to keep alive.

One thing the Devil said turned out to be true: Adam and Eve would know good and evil. That knowledge marked what we call "The Fall." It was a falling away from the presence of God, His peace and Sabbath rest. They stole knowledge fit only for God. Adam and Eve were overwhelmed and ruined as a result. Satan did achieve a victory from his point of view, but as every reader of the real Bible knows, the Devil's victory is limited and will not last forever.

The worst result of the Fall for the man and the woman was being forced to leave their home. The source of life, which was the Tree of Life, was in the garden. Henceforth, it was no longer available to them. They were sent away east of the Garden of Eden, and the path of return to the garden was blocked by God.

The man and the woman did not drop dead. In a sense, then, the Devil's words were true. The Devil is too clever to be completely wrong, so he employs a "lesser truth."

Yes, Eve and Adam did not die, at least not physically. The story in Genesis informs us that they went on to live a long time and to have at least three more children. Of the first two children born to them, one killed the other – Cain killed Abel. Added to fear, shame, concealment, and blame was envy, jealousy, and murder. The Devil's lies produced an abundance of rotten fruit.

Living east of Eden our original parents no longer had access to the Tree of Life, and the result was inevitable physical death at some point. Physical death is one thing; separation from God is another. Like Adam and Eve, we will all die, and then there is the judgment. Unless He himself repairs the breach, as in His provision of the perfect sacrifice in Jesus, separation from God is forever. That separation is spiritual death.

The Devil is not limited by the truth. One minute he will seek to convince us, as he did with Eve, that we will never die; the next minute he tries to convince us that physical death is all there is.

Chapter 2:
Eat, Drink, and Be Merry

All will agree to this time honored and wonderfully human saying that derives from one of YKW's books itself (you remember Solomon, don't you, who was the wisest of the wise): "Eat, drink, and be merry, because the grave is all there is."

The Devil's own commentary

I like food and grog with it — hopefully above 12 proof. Enjoying and savoring what we can stuff into our mouths and bellies, frolicking with abandon, relishing ribald humor, indulging our glorious sexual appetites with sweet young flesh. Yes, what a superb way to live! The earth yields up succulent delights galore, so why should we ignore them? Nothing that satisfies the senses should be beyond consideration. YKW put it all here, so surely we should take advantage of all these gifts. Indeed, I am a gourmet; I settle for nothing less than the best.

As for the verse itself, I borrowed it from YKW's detestable book, and after a brilliant edit it becomes a saying to live by. After all, Solomon, who was no less than the son of David and a man after YKW's own heart, is the author. If you *must* see the original, it is from Ecclesiastes 8:15: "And I commend joy, for man has no good thing under the sun but to eat and drink and be joyful, for this will go with him in his toil through the days of his life that YKW has given him under the sun." You see, it is not really that different from my own version.

It's likely that the phrase "life that YKW has given him" was added by some overzealous scribe and does not belong in the text. It should have read that *I* was the one who gave life and pleasure. Eating, drinking, and being merry is sexy. YKW would have us shrivel up and die, living the life of a celibate monk existing on bread and water.

If the grave were not the end, then all the eating, drinking, and being merry would not be sexy. But because it is, I advise you to let go and do it, and don't hold back, since there is nothing to lose.

• •

A Christian's response

In high school, my friends and I actually reasoned in much the same way. I hate to admit it, but I assumed that I would never live to age twenty-one, so I compensated by carrying on as badly as I could. What a mistake.

The Devil is a fallen angel without a digestive system, but he has a vivid imagination. Christians will eat, drink, and be merry. But that is not all we have.

One does not have to be a drunk or a glutton or a profligate to enjoy the natural pleasures. Maybe I have not tasted all the dishes Julia Child writes about in her cookbook, *Mastering the Art of French Cooking,* and I have not sampled all of the best Napa Valley wines, but I am making some progress in enjoying art, music, theatre, sports, and a good sex life with my wife.

Many of the most privileged people on earth learn that life is not about satisfying the self. Those consumed with self end up bored, fat, alcoholic, crazy, addicted, and ultimately depraved. The formulas of "Me, Me, Me" and "More, More, More" yield disaster and a failed life.

I am learning to be content with what is mine in this

flawed and temporary existence. Assuredly, this learning is a life-long process. What I have has been given to me, and it is more than enough: peace with God, forgiveness of my sin, the gift of eternal life, a meaning and purpose for living, the indwelling of God's Holy Spirit, the joy of the Gospel, and a strong hope for the future. In addition, I have the pleasure of God's revealing Himself to me in the Scripture; there is prayer, my talking with the Creator anytime or anywhere; there is fellowship with the people of God; there is music, art, and worship that belong to the whole Church. My life has not been ordinary since the transcendent, almighty God invaded my life by His grace and mercy through the Lord Jesus Christ. And, I have never been alone; I have not walked the dark paths without the light of Jesus shinning ahead of me.

Not that my life has been angelic. No, I have walked some places I ought not to have gone and have been challenged to my core on more than one occasion. In my heart and mind are regrets, remorse, and repentance. I have learned that "the kingdom of God is not a matter of eating and drinking but of righteousness and peace and joy in the Holy Spirit" (Romans 14:17).

The Devil wants us to believe that the grave is the end and uses the musings of King Solomon, who learned that life's toils and enjoyments are all from God the Creator. The Devil even admits that "the grave is all there is" is not a part of the original passage in Ecclesiastes. He even slips up and inserts his greatest fear: "If the grave were not the end..." As many experience, there is a part of me that fears the unknown and wishes for total annihilation after death, but when such thoughts come I can send them away speedily. God's plan pointed to Jesus' cross and resurrection, which confirm the great truth that those whom He has called will enjoy Him forever. This is the great and ultimate intention of God, and I am convinced He knows what He is doing.

The Devil wants you to believe that the grave is the end

and that you had better enjoy the brief and only life you have, because he doesn't want you to consider that if you follow his advice, you will sadly discover that the grave is *not* the end, but then it will be too late and eternally so.

Chapter 3:
The Grave is the End

Remember, the grave is the end. Experience as much of
life as you can. All that really matters is your happiness,
so get everything you can out of your short existence on
earth. Explore every choice and live free. You don't want
to miss out on anything. Yes, I say, these are truly words
to live and die by. Hear this, so you can enjoy the life you
have; hear it and do it. So says the wise one.

The Devil's Commentary

Somewhere in YKW's book it says, "You do not know what
tomorrow will bring. What is your life? For you are a mist that
appears for a little time and then vanishes." Even followers
of YKW are aware of how fleeting a life can be and how little
time there is to experience it. *My* followers make the most
or their time and are not afraid to get all they can. Too many
humans live worried, guilt-ridden lives. Since the grave is the
end, what difference does it make what we do? And just in
case some may be tempted toward a twinge of conscience
and may be thinking that my way is too self-centered, be
assured I have the very best in mind for my followers.

I usually advocate limiting behavior that would lead to
jail. A principle to live by is, "Don't get caught." On this subject, YKW and I differ greatly. Let us not be naïve. Everyone
cheats, lies, and grabs as much as they can for themselves.
It is not only the politicians who wheel and deal; everyone

does it. Don't play the role of victim; stand up for yourself and do unto others before they undo you. I am making every minute count, and so should you.

Lest you think that I have no guiding ethic, consider another of my doctrines: "Do not hurt anyone." That sounds nice. For the most part, those who have most thoroughly rejected the existence of YKW can live ethically balanced lives based upon well understood cultural norms, all the while determining for themselves what to do and what not to do without being bound by YKW's overarching commands. Some of my disciples live far cleaner lives than do a lot of the so-called "saints."[1]

Saints or no saints, most of the fun humans get to have involves substances and sex or combinations thereof. Now here is where there is room for creativity. You must live as you were born to be. You must do as you were genetically programmed. DNA works for more than linking suspects to crime; it provides a rationale for just about everything. Remember these words when you are unfairly accused: "I was born this way, so leave me alone. Don't discriminate against me. I have my rights." You have the right to behave as you were born. How can that be wrong?

Repression of basic needs and desires is not good for us. Love is what we need; love is what we have to give. It is what makes the world go 'round. How is love expressed? You determine that yourself. Love is something you feel. It is like impulses, desires, and drives, driven by hormones. Seize the moment and let go of what fetters you from being completely natural. Let Me re-emphasize: how you are is how you were born to be. Act on it and ignore the moralists who would limit your pleasure. Who created that DNA, anyway? Not Me, but YKW did it, and what YKW has done is always called "good" and "right."

---

1   The term "saints" refers to any born-again Christian and is not limited to the officially beatified deceased who have qualified for sainthood under the doctrines or traditions of a church organization.

How would we know if something is actually bad for us anyway? How would we really know unless we experiment? So try all the different kinds of sex you can. You might find something new and exciting. And try various substances like the designer drugs – expand the mind, paint outside the lines, and think outside the box. It is well known that some of the most applauded artists did their best work while quite out of their minds. Many painters, sculptors, musicians, actors, and writers have taken my counsel to heart and have earned great wealth and applause.

Here in my Bible I am giving you a way to enjoy the few short years you have. Every word comes right from my heart. It is my truth, and it can be yours as well. Your life is brief, and it will also be repressed and empty unless you reach out for as much as you can get. Ignore the rule-makers and the bible-thumpers, deny guilt, and be yourself. You are a lot more like Me than you might think.

• •

A Christian's response

Why is the Devil repeating this theme that the grave is the end? It is because the Devil is a liar, and his only interest is getting you to spend eternity with him in the nether regions – hell – rather than with the Lord God who is in heaven. This is the bottom line.

Don't be put off by my use of the word "hell." There may be a temptation to dismiss my responses, thinking that only nuts on the fringe use such apocalyptic terminology. And that would be so, if there were no reality to hell. However, consider the biblical view: hell was created for Satan and his demons; it is a place to which sin, death, and evil must be banished, since God is holy and no sin can possibly be in His presence. The Devil offers a few cheap thrills now and thinks that will blind his followers to the greater truth: They will be led directly to a miserable eternity and left to consider their terrible destiny forever.

Jesus knew the Devil, demons, and hell. He had personal experiences with all three. Now consider Jesus for a moment. No wrong was found in Him, no unloveliness displayed for a moment; He was always full of grace and mercy. He perfectly fulfilled in detail the dozens of prophecies spoken over the course of centuries then written in the Bible about the Messiah. Studying Jesus has led me to the conclusion that God indeed "became flesh and dwelt among us" (see John 1:14), all for the purpose of taking our sin, death, and hell upon Himself on the cross.

The passage the Devil quotes about life being "like a mist that appears then vanishes,"[2] must be approached with caution, because it is partly true. Our lives are short, and it is normal that we would want to experience to the fullest the life we have. It is a good thing I am a Christian and informed by Scripture as to what is right and good. If not, I admit I would fall victim to the crazy "wisdom" of the Devil. Especially when I was trying to be a beatnik, I was up to some real scary mischief. It was a form of self-focus that was a precursor to the hippie thing.

The satanic lie is that living our lives for maximum pleasure is the best we can hope for. But Satan is wrong on two points: one, the pleasures of the body and mind only go so deep before dissatisfaction and even boredom sets in; and two, God, our Creator, has better plans for us than we can imagine.

Additionally, everything has changed due to the Fall, as recorded in Genesis chapter three. There is little that can be called natural and normal anymore. Even down to the DNA level, biological life was corrupted by the tragedy that followed the rebellion in the Garden of Eden. The invasion of earth by Satan and his demons, and the fact that the human relationship with God was utterly broken, means that nothing will ever be the same until the day when God establishes

---

2   The verse is James 4:14.

among us His presence and His Kingdom. This is yet to come, but God's Kingdom may be partially seen in the Body of Christ, which is another name for the Church.

The Devil swears that the best a human can do is experience life, living to satisfy his or her feelings and natural drives. Is this right? How can we determine we are hearing the truth? Ask someone like me who has lived for himself and attempted to satisfy himself no matter who or what got in the way. Many Christians, even saints in the pews, would attest to doing this. The temptation to sin is powerful. Hormones have the power to push me around without mercy and led me to do all sorts of stupid things while utterly ignoring the dignity and personhood of others whom I tried to use in order to fulfill my lusts. This is not an exaggeration.

Guilt from sinning and following our feelings and urges without restraint severely impacts us mentally, physically, and spiritually. Guilt is an emotion and cannot be disregarded. If guilt is left unchecked and unforgiven, it will morph into anger, depression, fear, anxiety, and worse. Those who surrender to their sinful desires will experience guilt, no matter what rationalizations they embrace.

God has made us for Himself and not for the Devil. God has placed brakes within us intended to preserve our well-being. On top of that, and far more reliable, is the revelation of God's laws found in Scripture. The trouble is that when we go against both our conscience and the Bible, then guilt is the result. The usual way we try to avoid the torment of guilt is to ignore our inner compass and refuse to acknowledge God's revelation in Scripture. In fact, we will go to any lengths to prevent ourselves from facing the consequences of our lawless ways.

In John 3:19-20, Jesus said that people will do anything to keep their sinfulness from being exposed:

And this is the judgment: the light has come

into the world, and people loved the darkness rather than the light because their deeds were evil. For everyone who does wicked things hates the light and does not come to the light, lest his deeds should be exposed.

This is dramatic language and spot-on true. Alas, loving darkness is part of the human experience. We will hide from God, deny His truth, kill those who represent Him, and applaud those who follow the Devil's agenda. We killed the King of Glory when we nailed Jesus to the tree, and it must be "we," since Jesus died for *our* sin, and we are all guilty. We just don't want to admit it.

We should expect the Devil to urge sinful behavior, because it makes us want to hide from God, to fear Him, and to hate Him. How do you hide from God? By ignoring and rejecting those whom He sends to you. While dying on the cross Jesus prayed, "Father, forgive them for they do not know what they are doing." This prayer has been answered in my life. Maybe it can be answered in yours as well.

Chapter 4:
It's Nice to Be Nice

It is nice to be nice. Think positive thoughts. Do good deeds. When it is all over, you will be good enough to tip the scales in your favor. Be good, extend yourselves to help others, and never hurt anyone. You will then have nothing to fear.

The Devil's Commentary

Does not YKW say in his book that "faith without works is dead"? This is one of the few of his ideas we take seriously. Works are better than faith, as good deeds are evidence that faith is there. Being good means you believe, and this is entirely good enough.

Do good, be good, and all will be well.

A disciple came to Me one day and asked if she had to be nice to followers of YKW. My answer was, "Yes." Being kind and considerate is paramount. However, it is not necessary to like them.

Over the centuries my followers have reported that just being around those "saints" gives them feelings of revulsion. When I press them for details I hear things like, "I just want to get away from them," "I feel they are looking down on me," "It is like they are judging me," "They won't let me be me," and "It is all I can do to keep from striking them with my fists." I, Satan, reply that I have felt all this and more. Despite that, we must be nice and appear to be good and kind.

Remember: The road to heaven is paved with good deeds – that is, if there *were* a heaven. So in order to cover all the bases, be nice.

• •

A Christian's response

It could be argued that Satan's biggest lie is that what matters is doing good.

When I was in high school, a friend invited me help out at a school for the blind. He said there were parties, dances, and outings at the beach. For a whole year I did this and felt quite proud of myself, although in my heart was a lust for some of the girls. I tried and tried to fulfill this desire but never could get it done, due to my extreme ineptitude. I was a real mixed bag, with good and evil existing side by side.

We have seen on government buildings, such as a court house, the image of Justice holding a scale. This image is associated with God, who plays the part of a judge and holds a scale in His hand. On one side of the scale are placed a person's bad deeds and on the other the good deeds. If the good deeds outweigh the bad, magically that person gains entrance into whatever lovely place or state he supposes follows physical death.

When the Devil offers his slogans about good deeds, he tacitly admits to some kind of judgment, but one based on merit or the lack thereof. He is also suggesting that there is a possible negative outcome of our actions. Satan implicitly admits that there is a Power higher than himself, a Power with the right to judge.

Satan depends on people not being careful when considering his statements, which is why his book is so contradictory. The Devil knows that people who are looking for loopholes will grasp at anything in his bible, no matter how inconsistent. A favorite method of his is to find some kind of proof-text in the Creator's book, the real Bible, that might be used to support his argument.

James 2:17 says, "So also faith by itself, if it does not have works is dead." The Devil certainly knows this and has been able to *spin* the verse into meaning that doing good works is all that is necessary, and what is especially *not* necessary is faith in Christ's atoning death on the cross. Before I conclude my response to the Devil's spin, let us examine a few verses that follow the above quotation.

> But someone will say, "You have faith and I have works." Show me your faith apart from your works, and I will show you my faith by my works. You believe that God is one; you do well. Even the demons believe – and shudder! (James 2:18-19)

Works do not stand alone; they follow faith. Every Christian knows this. Because we are saved by grace, by means of the sacrifice of Christ the Lamb on the cross, good works result. Paul most clearly points this out in his letter to the Ephesians:

> For by grace you have been saved through faith. And this is not your own doing; it is the gift of God, not a result of works, so that no one may boast. For we are his workmanship, created in Christ Jesus for good works, which God prepared beforehand, that we should walk in them. (Ephesians 2:8-10)

That is about as clear as it could be. Paul had been a part of a religious system that informed him that his standing with God depended on his ability to keep the Law of Moses. The trouble was, Paul kept failing – over and over he failed, despite his best efforts. He knew that the Law taught that if he broke one of them it was the same as breaking them all. And he could never overcome his sinful nature. Breaking one law made him guilty and without hope.

But then, Jesus Himself appeared to him and rescued him

from all the sins he had committed. In addition to forgiveness of all his past sins, all the sin he would ever commit was also forgiven. How it can be that God cancels all our sin - past, present, and future - is a great mystery that runs counter to human understanding but is nonetheless a biblical truth.

Thus the Devil keeps broadcasting and preaching another system, one that is actually the oldest religious morality there is: be nice, kind, good, and positive. It sounds attractive, something that seems within a person's control, something that will bode well for whatever follows biological termination.

Good works are just that, but no more. People *seem* capable of being nice, positive, and good. However, is there an act that is totally selfless? Is there not always something in it for the doer? Some argue that pure altruism is unachievable, and that may or may not be true, but what is certain is that no good work, no matter how grand or how often it is repeated, will cover human law-breaking. It really is that simple. The Devil sounds good, but then so do most carefully crafted lies. And Satan has been at it longer than anyone else.

Chapter 5:
Celebrate Diversity
and Tolerance

To be contemporary we must celebrate diversity and learn to be tolerant. Be more progressive in your thinking and embrace the concept that all paths lead to YKW. Those who follow this more generous way of thinking are truly my disciples and always proclaim loud and long my version of wisdom and knowledge.

The Devil's Commentary

Have you seen my bumper sticker that says "C.O.E.X.I.S.T.?" Look closely at it and you will see symbols that make up the letters, each representing one of the major world religions. I commissioned that piece because it perfectly demonstrates the need for all people to get along with one another.

"Diversity" and "tolerance" are two of my favorite terms. They are culturally trendy in first-world countries and are easily embraced by followers of YKW because of their similarity to his admonition to "love your neighbor,"[1] which we know is impossible. It's not hard to show YKW's poor "wretches"[2] how narrow-minded, bigoted and hopelessly

---

1   See Leviticus 19:18; Matthew 22:38-39

2   "Wretch" – John Newton used the word in one of the hymns Satan hates the most, *Amazing Grace*. Wretch means not worthy and thus heightens the idea of grace, but many people change the word to obscure Newton's intent.

backward they've been, particularly since I have the full weight of cultural and political mandates behind Me. The merely "Christianized"[3] tend to see the truth quickly, especially when they are in front of friends and family. Some of them have very little backbone (I don't mean you, Dear Reader), and my advocates are expert at making them feel stupid, mean, and unloving, as well they should. After all, it's terribly narrow-minded and unloving to deny the validity of other religions, thereby condemning to hell billions of innocent people all over the world. I remind the little "saints" that the majority of the world's inhabitants cannot all be wrong, and we don't mince words. It's not a smear to call the exclusivists "elitist." It's the truth. The nerve of those Christians, thinking they have the only real deity!

I promote the veneration of diversity and tolerance as moral virtues, not to be muddied by discernment or making silly distinctions. It is evil to judge, so whole-hearted acceptance of anything and everything is the way to truly honor these lofty virtues. Those who insist there is only one way and only one book are deserving of belittlement. My followers side with Me every time, once they see that in doing so they can have that assurance of superiority over the ignorant and antiquated believers in YKW.

One of my current projects is teaching diversity and tolerance to elementary school children. Thanks to Me, political correctness is inculcated into the minds of the very young as they are taught the necessity of accepting every belief as being equally valid. The standard of truth is not right and wrong, but rather the degree of sincerity one brings to it. If you are sincere and believe with all your heart, then "it's all good," as they say. I am very pleased to see the schools

---

3   "Christianized" refers to those who are not "born again" and suppose they are actual Christians when they are not. The Christianized are those who think that, due to their religiosity, they are completely safe. They do not recognize they are perched on the very edge of the abyss.

and media doing so much of my work for Me, as they rein-force ideas of political correctness throughout society. Soon I hope to go further and promote acceptance of cherished sexual, so-called "perversions," by using the legal systems of democratic countries, mainly their hate crimes legislation and civil rights laws. Those laws are already in operation in some places, praise my name!

• •

A Christian's response

Tolerance is a virtue that Christians value; it is perfectly biblical. The tolerance of many, however, does not seem so very tolerant when one scratches just below the surface. One finds it is often limited to acceptance only of those who are like-minded.

Tolerance ought not to be blind acceptance. Everyone, whether they admit it or not, practices discernment accord-ing to some standard. Regarding religious doctrine, it is bet-ter for us to agree to disagree than to ignore or weaken our Christian precepts. Christians will disagree with those who hold anti-Christian views but not attempt to suppress those ideas or their followers. Mature, biblically-oriented Chris-tians do not feel the need to squash opponents, much less kill them. There have been instances when Christians have not lived up to the biblical ethic to love one's enemies. Nev-ertheless, the admonition of Jesus to love one's enemies remains as the highest standard of interpersonal conduct.

Christians do not expect adherents of other religions to accept as valid that all paths lead to the true and living God, and they certainly do not accept this themselves. Jesus said, "I am the way, and the truth, and the life. No one comes to the Father except through me" (John 14:6). If we believe that He is the only way to God, then we will not embrace the notion of many paths to God merely for the sake of political correctness or for any other reason.

I, a Christian, will not embrace laws that allow and promote behavior that is contrary to God's law. However, I will uphold secular law as best I can without compromising my God-given rights to protest and hold that such behavior is sinful. Tolerance must work both ways, because once a law contrary to Scripture is made, it can be used as a club to silence those in opposition.

Christians accept the concept of diversity. We live in the world with all its beauty and ugliness as citizens of the nations, fellow humans on the planet, yet pilgrims just passing through. It is a fallen world, having plunged far from the original intent of God. While Christians may be horrified at the deeds of those who glory in sin, we do not attempt to live in holy ghettoes. Though we live in this world, Jesus said that we are not of this world.

Christianity is incredibly diverse. Representatives of all races and all peoples are part of the household of God. Every nation and language on the good earth has its Christian expression.

But biblically faithful Christians will not accept excuses for sinful behavior. Some behaviors are not going to get the Christian seal of approval, and no apologies need be made.

Nevertheless, Christians are not always in agreement among themselves about some things. Homosexuality is one issue over which Christians are in some disagreement, but the majority understand that on a biblical basis, homosexual behavior is simply wrong. Genesis chapter one speaks of God creating both man and woman in His own image to "be fruitful and multiply."[4] Genesis chapter two speaks of the need of the man for a woman as a companion or helper.[5] The laws of Leviticus explicitly reject homosexual behavior,[6] as does Paul with the strongest language in his letters to the

---

4   See Genesis 1:27-28.

5   See Genesis 2:18-25.

6   See Leviticus 18:22 and 20:13.

Romans[7] and the Corinthians.[8]

Christians are tolerant, but we will not deny our strong sense of right and wrong. Despite the tendency of the world to shift in the wind and accommodate sin, we will not be moved from our Solid Rock. And Christians are diverse, but not to the point of accepting as valid all forms of behavior. Who could really claim to be completely tolerant and blind to differences? The devil's disciples work hard to undermine the biblical understanding of tolerance and diversity. Indeed, they extend their brand of tolerance to every group on the face of the planet except Christians. They have it backwards about who is "narrow-minded and bigoted."

---

7   Romans 1:24-27.

8   1 Corinthians 6:9.

Chapter 6:
That "Other" Bible is
Hopelessly Outdated

YKW's bible is hopelessly outdated, complicated, and
unintelligible to modern readers. Insist on consistency,
historical accuracy, and scientific verifiability! My disciples
will do this and thus are bound to reject any document
that has countless errors and is laughably naïve, relying
on miracles to explain what the ancient mind could not understand.

The Devil's Commentary

As for demonstrating that YKW's bible is hopelessly outdated, that is a simple task. That book is easy to discredit,
since hardly anyone understands it anyway, and many have
never read one page of it. Many "christianized" believers flat-
ter themselves that they are bible experts, but they have
only a superficial knowledge of it. All the better for Me.

Modern life and the modern attention span demand that
ideas be conveyed with simple, bold strokes and with pic-
tures. Who has time for such a voluminous tome as YKW's
bible? Who has an ancient Hebrew mindset to comprehend
archaic laws and tall tales, and what possible relevance
could it have for us in this day and age? Besides being complicated, that bible is not consistent, not factually accurate,
and not scientifically provable. No one living in the 21st century should be expected to take this thing seriously. One of

my favorite groups, the Je—s Seminar, does a great job of eliminating from that bible all the material about Je—s that indicates he could perform miracles, or claimed to be YKW, or could cast out my workers (whom he calls "demons") from their favorite homes, which are human beings, whether they realize the presence of my workers or not. Most modern people wisely disbelieve any of those old, outdated ideas.

Those who appear to have received some revelation in the words of that book are clearly locked in their own little world of delusion, because there is nothing in the book worth revealing. It is a muddy mess, and my best advice is to shut your eyes to it and don't even try to understand it.

• •

A Christian's Response

In the revealed Word of God, we read that "the god of this world has blinded the minds of the unbelievers, to keep them from seeing the light of the gospel of the glory of Christ, who is the image of God."[1]

In my junior year of college I took a Philosophy of Religion course from Professor Child at University of California at Davis. Our course project was a paper on one of the world's religions. Taking fifteen units at school and working forty-eight hours a week as a medic in the Air Force squeezed my available time, so I chose to write on Christianity, thinking I knew all about it and could knock out a paper quickly. Boy, was I wrong.

I picked up a Bible that my wife found and tried to read the first chapter of Genesis. It made no sense. I tried again a couple days later and got so frustrated that I threw the Bible against a wall and shouted that such a book should never be in plain sight again.

Unhappily, many are blinded and cannot make sense of the Bible and are then motivated to explain it away as merely a compilation of folk myths. Even while relegating

---

1   2 Corinthians 4:4

the Bible to the status of just another collection of religious history stories, people must still do something with Jesus. They must decide who He is. Instead of perceiving Jesus as the divine Son of God, they resort to diminishing Him into a personage who is easily dismissed – avatar, bodhisattva, guru, powerful and wise teacher, angel, holy man, religion founder, charlatan, magician, and so on. Most Christians are aware of how non-Christians view Jesus, since we all started out pretty much the same way. We were rebels against God, despising the truth and ready to believe any incredible explanation other than what is presented in the Bible.

For Christians, there comes a point when faith and love of God replaces our rejection and hate of Him; how that happens is a question we are unable to answer with any certainty. We have some ideas. Perhaps somebody prays for us; or we come to the conclusion that there must be something or someone responsible for the universe; or we are gripped by a sense of right and wrong when guilt floods in upon us; or we feel the despair that often accompanies a commitment to embrace a godless, pointless, meaninglessness existence. Perhaps we have experienced something more substantial, such as conversing with a Christian, reading a book that contains the Good News, hearing a musical composition with lyrics containing a biblical core message, or attending a Christian worship service where a faithful preacher of the Gospel presents the person and work of Jesus Christ.

A person whose eyes have been blinded by Satan cannot discern the work of the Holy Spirit, which points to Jesus and describes Him as true human miracle worker and true God, the Son of the Father. They must dismiss the Bible as outdated. They insist that it meet their scientifically verifiable criteria. They cannot accept a supernatural God. They dare not take God's Bible seriously, for it would require a complete change of mind. That complete change of mind is called "repentance."

The one whose eyes have been opened by the work of

God's Holy Spirit becomes empowered to discern spiritual things. That person suddenly finds in the words of the Bible the source of all truth and life, where previously they may have found only confusion. This transformation is part of the process of our reconciliation with our God, and the Holy Bible plays a critical part in that process.

Chapter 7:
Religion Is the
Main Cause of Wars

*rganized religion is the source of the world's suffer-
ing. Eliminate religion and there will be peace. The
worst religion for war-mongering has to be Christianity.
Consider YKW in his Old Testament. There you will discover a deity who seems to revel in war and murder. But don't
actually read it; just take my word for it, as do all my faithful disciples.*

The Devil's Commentary

Nearly every war was caused by religious zealots. In news
reports around the world every day, we read about religious
fanatics murdering members of some group or another, and
often their targets are other religious wackos. It is all over the
Middle East and in Africa, too. Religious wars happen every-
where. Religion has caused so much destruction, it really
should be made illegal. It is a relic of the past.

Imagine the waste of resources required to contain and
clean-up all the misery generated by the religionists. Imagine what it would be like to trash all the factious religions.
History records many conflicts between Orthodox, Cath-
olics, Protestants, and the other various sects. Don't forget
the independents and the cultists who fight everyone who
differs even slightly. Religion is also to blame for wars that
only appear to be political or economic on the surface, like

the Kosovo war or the various forays into Muslim Iraq and Afghanistan by Christian USA.

So what kind of a god is YKW? Murderous and trouble-causing from start to finish. How he got the reputation for being loving I'll never know. I don't see it and neither do those who follow Me. Loving has to do with letting people do what they want without constraint, fulfilling themselves, satisfying themselves. Live and let live! That is what I preach, and when the world follows Me, there will be peace.

• •

A Christian's response

It is a painful fact of history that religion is an element in causing wars. Religions have much to account for, and Christianity is no exception. I was troubled when I read about the Inquisition or the wars fought between "Christian" France, Spain, and England. Even the European/American wars, WW1 and WW11, were fought between so-called "Christian" nations.

It must be acknowledged that there has never been anything coming close to what might be called a "Christian nation." There have been countries that have been heavily impacted by Christianity, but raw power-politics was interwoven into the fabric that produced the conflicts between nations. Within national boundaries just in the last century, the majority of deaths was perpetrated not by those espousing religious ideals but just the opposite. Godless socialist, communist, and fascist regimes murdered tens of millions of their own citizens and the citizens of neighboring countries. Think of Hitler, Stalin, Mao, and Pol Pot, to name a few. In the midst of these conflicts there were always Christian voices in opposition, but they were few, weak, and silenced.

Christianity is a combination of both a visible and an invisible Church. The invisible Church is that population of true followers of Jesus Christ throughout the ages and around the world, called out by God himself. No one can see this invisible Church; it is observable only by God and will be so until the return of Jesus and the gathering of the "wheat from the weeds."[1]

It has always been so. Although Christians are a part of it, they are or should be aware of the twisted nature of the organized, visible Church. The visible Church can be radically compromised in this world. Jesus warned about it, as did New Testament writers like Paul, John, and Peter. The trouble arises from within the visible Church, which is public, meaning anyone might walk in the front door, including the Devil. Here is how Paul put it: "I know that after my departure fierce wolves will come in among you, not sparing the flock; and from among your own selves will arise men speaking twisted things."[2]

Christians have gone to war for various reasons, including the biblical warrant to obey the "emperor" or the "king." Christians are part of two kingdoms, the worldly and the heavenly, and obligations accrue from both. Conflicts will often arise, and the proper course is not always clear. Mistakes may be made when the conflict participants know of the biblical warrant to defend and protect family and freedoms. There is also biblical warrant to refrain from murder; thus we have conscientious objectors. Within the broad Christian community, differences surface as to the interpretation of the word "murder," which is the preferred reading over "kill," which is found in some versions of Exodus 20:13.

The invisible Church has never gone to war, since there is no authentic, invisible Church that could wage war. It was the visible Church that fought in the Crusades. Was it the invisible Church that engaged in war against Islam? No, it was a mixture of religion and politics. European Christians continually feared being overrun by Islamic armies. Some Crusades were driven by fame, fortune, and other evil desires

---

1   See Matthew 13:24-30.

2   Acts 20:29-30

that likely motivated those medieval kingdoms. Historically speaking, the Crusades cannot be laid at the door of the God of the Bible.

The Devil's accusations against God, blaming Him for making war as recorded in the Old Testament, are unfounded. The purpose of God must be seen in the judging of idolatry and perversion that characterized the Canaanite peoples who occupied the land promised to Abraham and his descendants. The strategy of driving out these peoples can then be viewed from a different vantage point. The God of Scripture is holy and righteous and will intervene in human history to judge it and make temporal corrections.

Imagine that organized religion was no more. Would the world then be peaceful? With a departure from faith in the God of the Bible, the enemy of God would fill the void without restraint. Would the Devil, who at his core is evil, murderous, and deceitful, usher in an era of peace and stability as he claims? If Satan were in charge, destruction and injustices would only increase. If that which restrains evil were gone, the lust for power would not disappear but would go unchecked. Wars and all manner of brutality would increase exponentially. And the Devil would rejoice, for death is what he seeks for us.

Chapter 8:
Believe in the Universe

You only need a higher power. There is no sense in personalizing faith. Be as broad as the Universe itself. Believe in the Universe, the grandest of all, the ultimate, which is truly infinite. When you believe in the material world, you believe also in Me, because I am actually the personalization of your basic material desires.

The Devil's Commentary

The Universe is a major focus of my religion, my "Perfect Path of Peace." My followers attain oneness with the Universe, because I am at one with it. So it was in the beginning, and it is far better to trust in the Universe than to believe in a god who might or might not have created it. The Universe has always been here and it always will be. The Universe is more than time and space; it is mind, soul, and spirit, and over it all I rule, including the principalities and the powers. Indeed, the answers to life's greatest questions are in the air, in deep space. Therein dwell the ancient masters who do my bidding.

The Universe is neutral, having no dos or don'ts. It frees you to follow your heart, so you only need to be true to yourself. When you make up the rules, no one can judge you, and no one may look over your shoulder.

The Christians talk about intelligent design as a proof for the existence of YKW, but what they ignorantly teach is nothing more than the basic nature of the Universe. We were born in the Universe, and we will die in it, and that is all there is. Believe in the Universe as you believe in Me, and your chances are increased for enjoying your short life in your little corner of the cosmos.

True religion, faith in the Universe, meets the test of logic; it is rational. Faith in a *personal* higher power is not logical; science shows this to be so. Now, since I am only the projection of your natural interests and longings, it is not inconsistent to believe in Me. I don't have to be tangible to be real.

• •

A Christian's response

The universe is grand in every way; after all, the Master Craftsman designed every atom of it. Scripture teaches, however, that the universe is not necessarily eternal.

People refer to the universe as though it were the ultimate reality. Some say it is personal and God-like. However, science hesitates to consider it everlasting. Some astrophysicists theorize that the energy and matter of the universe will collapse in upon itself and burn up, and others think it will drift apart and freeze out. In any case, it is wishful thinking to suppose that matter and energy will last forever. The Devil would have us take a further leap into fantasy to believe that the universe is not only eternal in terms of matter, but also a controlling entity with consciousness: the "Everlasting Mother."

What if science is wrong, and the universe actually had the capacity to continually renew or recycle itself? Would that mean anything to human beings? Satan presents a false hope by implying that the universe resembles a great mother who guides life processes. There is no consolation or nurturance in such a view. Neither is there any good science in what the Devil presents. In the universe we find only the Creator's original laws of physics at work, laws that hold no ethic or moral code and no concepts of right and wrong to inform us, guide us, or protect us. The universe has no heart and soul. It cares not for us.

The "Universe" is the new goddess of choice. The universe or creation has been spiritualized and personalized. It is another idol invented by the fantasy of humans. The sun, the moon, and the stars have been worshipped for eons. Perhaps more lives have been sacrificed to honor or placate the sun god than were killed in all religious wars put together. This kind of human sacrifice was practiced not only by the ancient Egyptians but also by the Aztecs of South America, among others.

The universe is merely that which God created. The creation or any part of it must not be worshipped, for that would be idol worship and errant.[1] When we pray we say, "Our Father, who is in heaven." Heaven and the universe are absolutely distinct in Christian doctrine. God "dwells" in heaven, and God in heaven created the universe.

The universe is not listening; it is neither person nor spirit, but it will come to an end. The Apostle Peter wrote: "But by the same word [of God] the heavens and earth which now exist are stored up for fire, being kept until the day of judgment and destruction of the ungodly" (2 Peter 3:7). That day of judgment, when it comes, will be like a thief in the night; it will come unexpectedly, and when it does, "then the heavens will pass away with a roar, and the heavenly bodies will be burned up and dissolved" (2 Peter 3:10). Peter got this understanding from Jesus who said, "Heaven and earth will pass away, but my words will not pass away" (Matthew 24:35).[2]

Satan says he is merely the projection of our base desires and longings, that somehow he is not tangible or actual.

---

1   The Sinai commandments, revolutionary in their time, continue to inform about the error of worshiping that which has been created instead of the Creator. See Exodus 20:3-4.

2   Also see Isaiah 34:1-2 and Revelation 6:14, 20:11.

But this is a contradiction. If he were nothing but thought, then he would not be a real being claiming the right to be worshiped or believed. But the Devil does crave worship, even if it is indirect and impersonal. The worship of an idol is essentially Devil-worship, since lurking behind the idol is a demon. The entity behind the mask of the worshiped object is Satan himself.

The God of Scripture, however, must be worshipped for who He is, and His attributes and character are disclosed in the Bible. There is no trickery and nothing hidden with the Triune God. What is revealed is that the God who created and controls the universe is the Judge of all. We will not last forever; we live for a short time, as even the Devil admits. Even if life lasted 120 years, death is still waiting for us. What Satan does not admit is that there will be a resurrection of every single individual, the just and the unjust, and it is a resurrection to judgment.[3]

At certain points in our lives, usually early on and before a measure of maturity is in place, we might rebel against restraints we find throughout the culture, especially those influenced or impacted by people holding the Bible as their standard for life. There is the urge to defy authority and to fulfill the desires of heart, mind, and eyes. It has even been said that the minds of humans are set on evil continually. The Devil hopes to capitalize on the natural inclination to "follow our hearts." Since the universe is not moral and cannot judge in the true sense, we are not accountable to the universe but rather to the Creator God.

It is probably not wise to look to the universe for answers. To place our faith and trust in that which will one day pass away is the worst possible error.

---

3   Examine the following passages on this issue: Daniel 12:1-2, Acts 24:15-16, Matthew 25:46, Romans 6:23, and John 5:24-29.

Chapter 9:
Unite with the One Soul

*W*e are all part of the One Soul, the Cosmic Mind, the infinite and eternal Spirit. All religions are a part of One Soul as are all members of every religion, whether they recognize it or not. My disciples know this and so value each and every person on the planet. We desire the upward way of peace and higher states of spiritual consciousness.

The Devil's Commentary

Differences between people are a superficial illusion. Look for common ground with others and embrace those who would not embrace you (unless they are followers of YKW – then you must revile them for their close-mindedness). This is the upward call of peace for those who choose to follow my way. Ours is the way of peace and love.

Our love is strong and broad. It includes those who are spiritually evolved and those who are not yet up to a mature spiritual plane. It is all a matter of timing. It may take many lives to rise to higher states of spirit consciousness.

Each individual is a microcosm reflecting the evolutionary ordering of the Universe, the macrocosm. When you look to Me, the Ultimate Soul, the Divine Mind, you unite with the One Soul that I perfectly embody. You can ultimately evolve into a divine being, having united the antiquated idea of a creator god with your own power to create.

Perfection comes from uniting your soul with all of creation, and my peace rises into the great Oneness. It positively blisses Me out to write about it, and I have found that oneness concepts work wonders, even better than walking on water. Didn't you feel the delight of enlightenment just by reading the passage above? Didn't it resound as mature, sophisticated, ethereal, and loving, especially in comparison to the narrow-minded and harsh teachings of the bible-thumpers?

Becoming spiritually evolved is a superior state of being within your grasp. Who can resist the draw?

• •

A Christian's response

Don't fall for the Devil's attempt to undermine timeless truths with high-sounding but faulty philosophical nonsense.

Christians may seem stuck in the past, since we hold to the tenets revealed in an ancient text.

However, our attention is focused on the beginning when God revealed Himself to the first humans, then on to the time of Moses, the Law, the prophets, and finally to the perfect time when He became flesh and lived among us, full of grace and truth. We also look forward to a time when God's Kingdom will be fulfilled in all its perfection. It is that focus that matters, not what goes around, comes around, or evolves.

After reading and thinking about this part of the Devil's bible, I decided to visit a local store that sold esoteric and mystical kinds of books. Initially I thought that the Devil was making things up, that people could not possibly believe such wild ideas. I was wrong. Many shelves of books about the very sort of thing I have been responding to in the last couple of chapters were arranged right in front of me. I knew I needed to take a closer look at some of that material. My conclusion is that the Devil has been successful at deceiving many more people than I originally imagined.

The idea that all things evolve toward that which is bet-

45

ter is patently untrue. Technologically we may be more advanced, and perhaps the surroundings of many humans are more comfortable, but spiritual conditions are another issue. Wars have not ceased, rather they have grown more numerous and deadly. Greed has not disappeared; indeed, corruption flourishes unabated. The planet has been ravaged to a level of toxicity that could not have been imagined a generation ago. Sexual perversity has become the new normal. The rates of addiction to alcohol and drugs have grown so much and so rapidly that our health care systems are overwhelmed. Our prisons are full, and we cannot build new ones fast enough.

Instead of being horrified at it all, we find more and more people approving self-gratification, such that it escalates to levels that even undemocratic governments are unable to control.

There does not exist "one" universal spirit, mind, soul, or consciousness. Such ideas form the foundation of Monism, which is the doctrine that only one supreme being exists and all the substance in the universe is unified in it. It is the concept behind Hinduism and religions that have spun off from it. Monism, one-ism, as in "one" spirit and so on, is surely the Devil's own concept, because it creates a false picture of reality.

The God who created all things existed before He created the universe, and He exists apart from His creation. God Almighty is the first and the last and is King of kings and Lord of lords. Because of Him we exist and it is to Him that we are accountable. It is His will that will be done, on earth and in heaven. God alone is eternal and infinite, and He is the great Judge of all. We will all stand before Him on that great and Last Day. All the high-sounding, liberal, and generous conglomerations of words will not change the fact that we will all be judged.

If the Devil's religion sounds good to you, it is an indication that you are headed the wrong way. If your flesh exults in his proclamations and your mind is numbed by the empty words of the Devil's bible, it is evidence that you have entered through a wide gate that opens onto the easy way that leads to destruction. Sadly, most go the way of the world; it is the most seductive direction to take when all paths are said to lead us to God or lead us to *become* gods. For your own sake and for the sake of God, listen to what Jesus said:

> "Enter by the narrow gate. For the gate is wide and the way is easy that leads to destruction, and those who enter by it are many. For the gate is narrow and the way is hard that leads to life, and those who find it are few." (Matthew 7:13-14)

Chapter 10:
Do Not Condemn Others to Hell

If you believe in the so-called "Son of YKW," then you are condemning to hell others who do not believe as you do.

The Devil's Commentary

Let Me explain: There is no hell, but if there were, and if you were a follower of YKW's supposed son, then just by believing in him you would be guilty of consigning your unbelieving family and friends to that imaginary place. We know that hate crimes start in the mind. What you believe has the power to create reality. This makes perfect sense, doesn't it?

Who brought up hell to begin with? Certainly not Me. Well, YKW's so-called son did and quite frequently. Make no mistake; the "good news" is not all about love and peace. Don't waste your time trying to investigate for yourself; you can trust Me on this. The one you *can't* trust is that mere bag of flesh who arrogantly calls himself the "son of YKW."

Once more, there is no hell, but if there were, I would be there with you, along with many others just like us. According to YKW's book, hell was created for Me and my followers, the fallen angels. How could angels be bad? Even if you think you should cover all the bases and believe that hell exists, take comfort in considering that the whole crowd there would just be having fun with Me.

The best idea is to deny hell. Then it won't exist. But believe in hell or don't; I win either way.

• •

A Christian's response

A few chapters back, I glanced ahead and saw this chapter was coming up. I do not like dealing with the concept of hell; in fact, I hate it and would rather avoid it. To think that people would go to that awful place forever horrifies me, just as it does all Christians. I wish it would just go away, but it won't. It is one of those things Christians are stuck with. I anticipate that the average reader's reaction will be one of revulsion, which is to be expected. I guess the best I can do is ask you to give this section a fair chance.

The Devil's twisted arguments naturally result in confusion. His attempt at making a logical argument in this passage about our Christian beliefs supposedly having the power to condemn others to hell is so absurd that it is difficult to make an orderly rebuttal of it. Of first importance is what is found in the Devil's commentary, which is something he slipped in that demands to be countered.

Who is Jesus?

The central issue has to do with Jesus, who is indeed the Son of God. That term actually refers to Jesus as the Messiah or Christ; the terms, Son of God and Son of Man, are like code words for Messiah or Christ. During the New Testament period this is how the Jews understood those terms. The Devil is counting on the human tendency to reject anything that seems illogical, and he also assumes our ignorance when it comes to biblical terminology.

I have a son, and he is human like I am. However, we do not have the same mind and will; we are two different people. But God the Father and God the Son are of the same essence, being, will, and mind, and they both pre-existed creation. Scripture uses the Father/Son metaphor to help us understand the great mystery of God.

49

The Son of God, Jesus, is eternal; there was never a time when He was not. This is what John meant when he wrote: "In the beginning was the Word, and the Word was with God, and the Word was God" (John 1:1). The verb "was" in the verse is a verb of being, imperfect-indicative in form, and lacks the concept of time. The English word "was" is past tense and does indicate time. However, Greek grammar demands we understand that the Son was and is the Word, the Son was and is with God, and the Word was and is God. This is the intent of John's sentence. There was a moment in time, a special *kairos* (Grk.) when the Word became flesh and dwelt among us (see John 1:14). Paul put it like this: "When the fullness of time had come, God sent forth his Son, born of woman, born under the law" (Galatians 4:4).

The New Testament teaches beyond question that Jesus is God. Consider this:

> He is the image of the invisible God, the first-born of all creation. For by him all things were created, in heaven and on earth, visible and invisible, whether thrones or dominions or rulers or authorities – all things were created through him and for him. And he is before all things, and in him all things hold together. And he is the head of the body, the church. He is the beginning, the firstborn from the dead, that in everything he might be preem-inent. For in him all the fullness of God was pleased to dwell, and through him to recon-cile to himself all things, whether on earth or in heaven, making peace by the blood of his cross. (Colossians 1:15-20)

Jesus is the Messiah or Christ promised by the prophets in the Old Testament. Many centuries before the birth of Jesus in Bethlehem, the prophet Isaiah said, "For to us a child is born, to us a son is given; and the government shall be upon his shoulder, and his name shall be called Wonderful Coun-selor, Mighty God, Everlasting Father, Prince of Peace" (Isaiah 9:6).

The testimony of Scripture is clear: Jesus is the eternal Son of God and He is God Himself.

What about hell?

Hell is just. Since God is holy and no sin can come before Him, then sin must be put away, and that includes sinners. Satan will indeed be in hell and so will his followers, the fallen angels or demons.[1]

Hell is not a good place. The Scripture describes hell as a place of darkness, punishment, and torment, without love and without God, and yes, full of fire and brimstone. No one escapes from hell, as Jesus made clear in a parable: "Between us and you a great chasm has been fixed, in order that those who would pass from here to you may not be able, and none may cross from there to us" (Luke 16:26).

Hell is forever. And it does not go away just because some-one does not believe in it. No one has authority over God and His creation. The Devil is ridiculous when he tries to insin-uate that humans have the capacity to create an opposing reality by disavowing God's reality. Probably most readers of his bible understand this and do not give any credence to his nonsensical concepts, but some will take any means of comfort they can find, no matter how implausible.

Club hell?

Just in case you imagine that hell exists and that you and your friends or relatives might end up there, Satan wants you to take comfort in knowing you will all be together partying on. In reality, there will be *no* party in hell. Hell is a place of loneliness and darkness. You may ask: "What about the light the fire makes?" The phrase "fire and brimstone" does not

---

1   See Matthew 25:41 and 2 Peter 2:4.

necessarily have to be taken literally. It is more of an idiom, a figure of speech, perhaps taken from Genesis 19:24, wherein God rained down "sulfur and fire" on Sodom and Gomorrah. Thus, the idea is that hell is an awful place. *Gehennah* is the word in the Greek New Testament that is translated into the English word hell. *Gehennah* was a real place, a shallow valley called *Hinnom* that ran just beyond the southern wall of Jerusalem and was used as a garbage dump. Fires continually burned there to consume the waste from the city. It became a convenient metaphor for speaking about that which was indescribably awful.

Cartoons in newspapers often employ images of heaven and hell that are based on fantasy and imagination rather than reality. No one knows what hell really is, but some reliable facts are these: hell is eternal, Satan rules it with his demons, sin will be there, but God will certainly not be there.

Heaven is the presence of God, and His holiness permeates it. It is ultimate glory, the uninterrupted and eternal rest in God and fellowship with Him.

Condemning to hell

A major mistake the Devil makes is to insinuate that we have the ability and power to condemn anyone to hell with our beliefs. But whether or not I believe in heaven or hell determines no one else's destiny.

The fact is that we are condemned to hell because of our sin. We have broken God's law, and the result is an eternity in hell. Sin cannot come into the presence of God, so to be with Him we must have our sin removed. And this is exactly the reason Jesus died on the cross. All the believer's sin was placed upon Jesus, no matter when in time a person lived. And as Jesus was buried, so our sin was likewise buried. All of our sin is removed from the judgment of God forever. This removal of our sin is due to God's good pleasure, which is why we use the word "grace" in speaking of the Good News or Gospel. Grace means a gift freely given, without being earned even to the slightest degree. Picture a person, guilty and condemned to hell, suddenly and dramatically rescued from going there.

The Devil's purpose is to take as many as possible with him to this ultimate destination. God's purpose is to rescue sinners from the awfulness of hell. This is what it is all about.

Chapter 11:
Christianity is for Losers

Don't identify with the Christians; they have lost the cultural battle and are nothing but a despised minority. It is not cool to be a Christian.

The Devil's Commentary

If Christians were the people of a powerful god, they would be doing much better than they are. How much time do they need? Two thousand years in the new era and two thousand years in the old era, and where have they gotten? Theirs is not a success story.

Sure, there are some grand buildings, and yes, there have been some intellectual achievements, if you count notoriety among the deceived as achieving anything. But today they are losing out. Look at the statistics. In places where they once flourished, like most of Europe and even their stronghold, America, their numbers show a marked decline. If the whole thing were owned by a real god, how could it be anything but upward and onward? But you wait and see. *My* people will come to the forefront, and Christians will be in continual retreat, to the point that it will even be dangerous to be one of them. They sound mighty and big while they are in the majority, but just wait; they will run for cover when they are few and powerless.

Cool? Christian is not cool. Every once in a while a real bad apple ends up in their hands, and then they love to parade the x-profligate around giving a testimony of the wonderful change that occurred since they found religion. But if you have been paying attention, I get some of these back, and if not, then I make them sound like the crazies they are. Now the Devil is cool. Satan, with my dark, deep mysteries and thrills is way cool!

• •

A Christian's response

Much of the above is true, which increases the chances that the Devil's deception will be believed. Clearly, every Christian, though a follower of Jesus, has a fallen nature. Even in the New Testament, Christians were flawed people, including Peter and Paul. There is no attempt on the part of the Bible authors to portray Christians as angelic or without the capacity to sin. Therefore, it is easy to trash Christians. However, look at Jesus and study Him, and you will see something else. Believers in Jesus are slowly growing up into the measure of His stature, and it is a life-long process.

Identifying with Christians can indeed be dangerous. Every day Christians lose their lives and are raped, robbed, and pillaged for no other reason than that they are Christians. In most of America it is still safe to confess Christ publically, but this could change. It has never been easy to stand and say, "I am a follower of the Lord Jesus Christ." Rejection, ridicule, and much more may quickly follow. Only by God's grace are we able to stand at all.

The Devil will win some major victories as the end of history nears. Jesus made this clear just prior to His arrest and crucifixion. He said lawlessness will increase, that there will be great tribulation, and false christs and false prophets will perform great miracles and lead many astray.[1] Right now the power of Satan is being restrained; it will be released at some unknown point, which will result in Satan gaining some ground, to the extent that he publically proclaims

---

1   See Matthew chapter 24.

himself to be God.[2]

Christians, including those who adhere to a biblical theology, have indeed been decreasing in numbers in America as well as in Europe, which has slid much farther down the slippery slope to secularism and atheism.

This phenomenon has happened before. Prior to each of America's great awakenings, abandonment of Christian practice and principles has been documented.[3] If God did not periodically pour out His Spirit and fill up the churches with new converts, Christianity would likely disappear in time. Because the visible Church is a human institution, it is flawed and even corrupt, especially when it attempts to operate as other human organizations do.

It is certainly the case that on many fronts Christians are losing cultural battles. Consider the growing acceptance of abortion, homosexuality, and so on. This is nothing new. Jesus was quite clear that genuine Christians would be few. He also warned first century churches in Asia (now Turkey) that they would be hard-pressed to resist the teachings of immorality that surrounded them and that threatened to penetrate into the church community.[4]

If genuine Christians are decreasing in number and lawlessness is on the increase, how are we to measure success? Numbers, money, influence, power, and prestige are of the world, and as the Apostle John pointed out, "The world is passing away along with its desires." The ending of that verse makes all the difference: "But whoever does the will of God abides forever."[5]

Rejecting Jesus and being consumed by the lusts and

---

2   See 2 Thessalonians 2:1-12.

3   For a full discussion of this, see *Awakenings in America and the Jesus People Movement*, available at www.evpbooks.com.

4   See Revelation 2:18-29.

5   1 John 2:17.

pleasures of the world is not so cool in the long run. Appearances are deceiving. So, if a person gets all he wants and dies anyway, since no one gets out of this alive, all he can expect is to face judgment and hell. Hell is not cool. Abiding forever is cool.

Chapter 12:
Focus on Mother Earth
and the Environment

*W**hat counts is the Community of Earth. Personal salvation is self-centeredness to the extreme. Our mission must be focused on Mother Earth and all her children, from rock and hill to plant and animal. Do not rest until all species are treated equally. Our goal is universal salvation for all species, not just a few humans.*

The Devil's Commentary

The Christians always want to know what they can do to have salvation. How selfish! Where is the broader concern? Where is their love for all creatures, great and small? I'll tell you: there is none. The religionists don't care about what happens to their home, Mother Earth. They presume to be a higher species, and they rest in comfort while other animals suffer. They use and abuse, pillage and rape the whole planet, from the depths to the heights, from the ground to the air they breathe. They really care nothing about the pain of others, whatever species they may be. It is nothing less than selfishness, and personal salvation is all they think about: me, me, me.

The whole creation story in that unbelievable book called Genesis suggests humans were created special or different in some way that is almost godlike. How could *that* be? No, from one cell all life emerged, which slowly evolved into the myriad of species we have now. Mother Nature did it all. Billions of years of evolution have brought everything to the perfectly high state we see now. Science has shown this to be true. What a wonderful mechanism! No creator needed; no so-called intelligent designer. No preference for one species over another. No human care of other "lower" species like that other bible teaches. Humans, by the way, showed up so much later; it's ludicrous to think they ever had any "stewardship" over the rest.

My followers have a higher calling to nurture the environmental community, one that is utterly inclusive, with each unit of equal value. All life and the whole interdependent system is precious. Hills and plains, seas and streams are full of life, each necessary to the other. The Community of Earth and Oneness of life is our focus. Our Mother is the Earth, and She must be cared for and protected. I say recycling and resource conservation are better than caring for the decrepit, poor, and sick humans, who should be weeded out by the natural process of survival of the fittest. Now it's time to acknowledge that humans owe their whole existence to our Mother Earth, and they had better bow down and pay her homage. After all, She is my consort.

· ·

A Christian's response

This is a tricky issue. The devil insinuates that Christians are of one mind when it comes to how God did His creating. Actually, we do not all agree on this subject. I can see merit in what is termed Intelligent Design and even Theistic Evolution. At present I hold to both, however illogical that may seem. I accept the biblical account that God is the Creator, but about how long ago that happened and by what mechanism He accomplished the task, I have no opinion. I find the whole topic interesting but not of prime importance. Please feel free to disagree with me on this point, yet I am hoping the bulk of my commentary will be acceptable.

Personal salvation is a concern of extreme importance, since it is the difference between heaven and hell. Our Creator has planned a restored relationship between Him and His special creation, humankind, whom He created "in His image."

Christians can be selfish; in fact the biblical commands often assume our natural bent toward loving only ourselves. So the Devil is right about one thing: Christians will be selfish. However, we are called to turn from our selfishness to love God with all we are and have and to do the same toward others, whether friends or enemies.

The Devil insinuates that Christians ignore their home, planet Earth. Surely many have, in an effort to survive and out of ignorance, but sometimes due to a lack of care and concern. This has not been my personal experience, and there is nothing in Scripture nor in any Christian creed or confession of faith that commands or promotes abusing the natural world, either directly or indirectly.

Are all Christians engaged in harming the environment? Of course not. Though a Christian-oriented or heavily influenced culture has undergirded many industrial and technological advances, all of the abuse of the earth did not come at the hands of Christians, and is it certainly not part of the biblical agenda. But the Devil would have us think it is.

The Devil's accusations belong on his own head, because he has no real care or concern for the environment except as a ploy to make his followers think he shares an interest they have. It is indeed right to care for the planet, and each part is indeed intertwined with the whole. However (and it is a big however), this planet and the entire universe are temporary. A current scientific debate argues whether the universe will collapse and burn up or drift apart and freeze out; either way, time and space are not infinite. God alone is infinite, and His Kingdom is forever and ever. Concern for the universe is what philosophers call penultimate, not ultimate. Only the will and purpose of God is ultimate. God does not dwell in His creation. He was before there was a universe, and He will be forever. After all the atoms are dissolved, God is.

As we realize that God is above and beyond created space, time, and matter, the command to love God above all things does not seem strange or out of proportion. The quest for God is completely natural and normal; it is actually the opposite of self-centeredness. To be focused only on what is, while commendable to a degree, is a form of idol worship, which is to adore and honor the creation above the Creator.

As for ignoring the pain of others, there is no evidence for such an assertion. It is beyond the scope of this piece to recite the contributions Christians have made toward the wellbeing of people and other species in need. These efforts have been and continue to be enormous and need no defense. It is a case of the Devil's telling a big lie often and loud enough that some will believe it.

Chapter 13:
You Are Who You Are

You are who you are. It is impossible to change that. Therefore, be proud of who and what you are and take great pleasure in it. Come out of the closet!

The Devil's Commentary

Popeye was right, "I am what I am." Isn't this true? Of course it is!

This is not my first time around on this subject and it won't be the last. This is where we live and move and have our being: expressing ourselves, being who we really are, doing that which gives us pleasure. *They* call it "sins of the flesh." But if you know nothing about it, then you must not condemn it.

The Gay Pride events around the globe are a perfect model. Lift high the rainbow banner! Ignore the narrow-minded bigots. They have no right to rule your life anyway. You are how you were born to be, so shout it loud! Shout it on the streets! Shout it in the courts!

The old hippies of the 1960s had it right: "If it feels good, do it." Remember, I taught that to them, and what a time we had – drunk, stoned, and stupid. Consider another slogan that one of my spokesmen, Timothy Leary, used to twist minds and capture souls: "Turn on, tune in, and drop out." Some are still following my wise words.

To my homosexual and bisexual followers I say, be proud of who you are and what you do. I know you can feel the growing pride. Reveal the real you, and experience the pleasure that will erase years of denying yourself, especially since consenting acts hurt no one, right? Come out of the closet and stay out, celebrating your true identity!

• •

A Christian's response

The Devil obviously has a reason for his constant promotion of living for pleasure. He knows sin is fun for a season, but in the long run it is empty and cannot deliver contentment. A lie that encourages pleasure-seeking will be believed by some gullible people to the point that they become addicted and need ever-increasing stimulus to maintain. Living for oneself may be trumpeted by many, but it obscures the real reason for our creation, which is to know and glorify our Creator.

Our bodies are filled with nerves that respond to stimuli, some of which are pleasurable. Additionally, hormones are given by God for all kinds of good reasons, and some provide good feelings. Two sources can help us determine when we have taken pleasure-seeking too far. One is the Scripture, and the other is our conscience. The Scripture is more reliable, because our conscience is vulnerable to outside influences, such as what other people believe and practice. People have a tendency to move toward that which feels good, and following the will of God does not always feel good.

Satan's kingdom is not a place anyone would want to be, if the facts about that kingdom were known. It is a place of gnashing of teeth, darkness, loneliness, and torment, where one is subject to the whims of that which is absolutely evil. The Devil is no one's buddy and no one's friend, and demons do his bidding. Imagine the worst horrors that have been inflicted on humankind, and you begin to scratch the surface of what awaits those in Satan's kingdom.

Youthful bravado and rebellion, perhaps accompanied by anger and hatred, may cause many to take my Christian views of hell lightly, as though the Devil's kingdom were only a trifle. Not so! It is the lake of fire, the pit of death, and it lasts forever. Once a person is thrown through the gates of hell, he or she never leaves. Evil replaces love and joy; terror reigns in place of peace and security; hate rules instead of companionship and friendship. This is the nature of the eternal existence that awaits those who celebrate sin and are proud of it.

We are susceptible to the sins of the flesh, so who will cast the first stone? Christians and our Lord do not delight in pointing the finger in an attempt to shame and castigate. Just the opposite. Love demands telling the truth and warning of disappointment, dissatisfaction, damaged conscience, ruined lives, mental and physical deterioration, and the hell to come. Love points to the Savior who alone can deliver from this death and bring us into the kingdom of light and grace.

I speak on the basis of personal experience and what I have learned over four decades of pastoral ministry, which is that Jesus' followers experience more of the pleasures of the flesh than those who throw themselves into sinful practices. Mature Christians, I have come to find out, are some of the sexiest people on earth, because marriage between a man and a woman is the relationship for which God created sex. Any other context is unnatural and thus inferior. The sexual experience is substantially diminished when guilt and shame are added to the mix.

Narrow minded? Maybe some of us are or were narrow in our views, especially early on in our born-again[1] lives, but we grow up and relax our early tendencies toward legalism. Our

---

1   "Born-again" or more accurately, "born anew" is an action of God whereby a person's sin is forgiven, past, present, and future, he or she is indwelt by the Holy Spirit, placed into the invisible Church, and adopted by God as a son or daughter. *Conversion, regeneration*, and *saved* are synonyms for the same thing.

real passion is to present a Savior who loves us in spite of ourselves. Christians can talk about sin, when hardly anyone else will. This is because Christians are completely forgiven of our past, present, and future sins. Having been delivered from death and hell, we can talk about them without anxiety or fear. To some, that ease makes us scary, yet that is not our fault. We are who we are, but rather than being proud about it, we are thankful.

Chapter 14:
Bliss Out - Express
Your Emotions

Feel the spirit. Let go of your mind. Follow your feelings, urges, and hormones. Be awash in the bliss of your emotions. This is the place I inhabit.

The Devil's Commentary

True living means letting your emotions go free. Express yourself! Everything you experience through your senses and your raw, emotional responses is valid for you. Respond to the beating of a drum, or the crescendo from a wailing lead guitar, or the steady single note chanted until it breaks through. Sway or dance wildly and let the music take you to places beyond this world. Join with other revelers in life and make spiritual harmony. Float in the ethereal zone of bliss.

Our feelings and sensations are what drive us, and that is as it should be. They allow us to be our natural selves. We must act according to how we feel at any given moment, because we know what is true by how we feel.

Christians think too much. They like to constantly argue about their doctrines. They live in their heads and ignore their emotions. *My* Bible is uniform and simple. It is really all about the individual's natural inclinations and feelings. If you submit to the will of YKW, who only wants to box you into an impossibly tiny square, you will lose your freedom to be what you feel.

Who wants to be a religious robot? And who wants to be a slave to authoritarian and arbitrary laws and regulations? If laws impede your expression of bliss, work to change them. Picket and protest for your rights of freedom of speech and freedom of assembly, even freedom to be completely natural in the nude (as the progressives in San Francisco allow). I and my followers are progressive, and we reject anything repressive. And we will sue anyone who dares to take a stand against us. There is always a way to get at them.

But I digress. Remember, your personal bliss is what is important.

• •

A Christian's response

Our feelings, emotions, bodily drives, and hormones are all gifts from the Creator God. Sex is a pleasure God has given us. But who is sexually satisfied? Whose feelings yield comfort? It seems sometimes as though our bodies are our enemy, and our attempts to feel good betray us.

Why is this? The Bible tells us that a terrible and tragic thing occurred a long time ago. The first humans thought they knew better than God. They disobeyed Him, and everything changed. Sex was one aspect of their lives that was impacted severely. Adam and Eve, who had been having plenty of good sex and were always naked were then filled with guilt and shame and tried to hide from God. Nothing has changed from that day to this one.

It looks like the Devil is interested in creating addicts. Examine what he says: Follow your feelings and emotions, your urges and hormones. If these were all they should be and we all had a relationship with God based solidly on love, then we could follow that which is "natural" and be safe. However, "natural" impulses, the ones God gave our parents in the Garden of Eden, have been perverted ever since, and we can never trust them again. That is why God has said NO

67

in His laws, which are sometimes also reflected in the laws of human societies.

Addiction is part of our human experience. We try to fill the void in our hearts and minds with dope, sex, shopping, music, gambling, whatever, only to end up unsatisfied. The fun of "blissing out" is always short-lived, because we humans are the common denominator, and we are deeply flawed. We get confused about our real needs and think that more and more and more, ad nauseam, will be the answer. We find that we have cooked ourselves in glut, however slowly.

Chapter 15:
I Will be Your Closest Friend

If you come to me, I will provide everything you need. I will be in you and you in me. You will never be alone. I will comfort you, even entertain you. And I will give you powers that will amaze others and attract them to you. You will be widely known because of the wonderful gifts that I will give you. I'll make you a deal you can't refuse.

The Devil's Commentary

When I make a bargain, everyone gets a great deal. I give to my followers and they give to me. My gifts are supernatural, powerful, and awesome. Invite me into your life, and I will come to you.

YKW may invite you, too, but I am more fun and will not place unreasonable demands on you. With me there is nothing to give up and no straight path to follow. I make it all easy.

I am in tune with the highest stratum of people, those who are the real movers and shakers. My followers are the chief power-brokers; those who make the big decisions move at my direction. They always have access to me and my vast knowledge for consultation. My followers and I work together, and I provide all they need.

In fact, I am so closely intertwined with many of my followers that they could not carry on their lives without me. I am in them, and if anyone tries to "cast me out," I just come back stronger. (Even if I were "cast out," which is highly unlikely, my followers would sense a great void in their lives without me and quickly invite me back in.)

• •

A Christian's response

The devil does give gifts, which, for a period of time, seem to satisfy. He is able to produce supernatural signs and wonders, mimic heavenly encounters, and even appear as an angel of light. When Satan provides a venue for his disguised minions, the demons, to let loose their occult talents, we might be seduced by the thrill and covet the power and knowledge we see displayed. Many have been lured into the Devil's camp when they discover a spiritual world filled with all sorts of strange but tangible entities. When this happens, the bargain is struck.

However, the Devil's followers usually do not read the fine print when they make their deals with that crafty snake. Many do not even know that the deal they are making is with Satan, otherwise they would be more cautious.

The lures of the Devil's tricks are tangible power and knowledge, but they come with a price no one can pay. For a short while the Devil seems to be playing fair, being friendly, providing a new world of excitement, satisfying even perverse desires. Then, little by little, a change takes place. There is an expiration date on the Devil's gifts, and when that point is reached, the Devil demands his "pound of flesh." When you make a bargain with the Devil, beware! He loves to make a deal then unilaterally change the rules. Your contract looks good at the outset, but sooner or later you realize you have signed yourself over to destruction.

I have personally seen this very thing. A gift is given, let us say, to enable one to predict someone's future or describe events that happened in a person's past history. Maybe the gimmick involves sex and the power to have sex with people who would ordinarily be out of the question. Often the gifts are curses or spells, whether for good or evil, but down the road the so-called gift turns ugly. Often things happen that permanently and tragically alter a person's future. My thirty years as a volunteer at San Quentin Prison has proved this to me over and over.

Chapter 16:
I Give Power-Gifts and Miracles

Now I will let you know more of the great and powerful gifts I have to give you that are unlike any that YKW would give. If you seek Me, if you worship Me, then miracles unparalleled will be yours, and you will be mine.

The Devil's Commentary

Even in *that* book which mocks Me, it is admitted that I am the Ruler of this World and the Prince of the Power of the Air.[1] I can take your body over and provide experiences beyond belief. I can take you places and give you knowledge and experiences that are superhuman. It is stuff that YKW would never give to you. I am not boasting. Miracles are common for those who follow Me.

My miracle religions are old and honored by millions. How could they be wrong? I have countless fortune tellers, shamans, santeros, witches, warlocks, magicians, wizards, mediums, psychics, and more. From ancient times, I raised these up to be my ministers and priests. They do my bidding and receive my power, and I give them control over health, love, and money. I am present in their rites and rituals; I am present in the magick circle, the trance and pathworking, and in the tambor, bembe, asiento, registro, and cowrie shells of Santeria. I inhabit the séance, the Ouija board, and the crystal ball; I speak through the medium, the astrologer, the

---

1   See John 12:31 and Ephesians 2:2.

channeller, and the psychic. (Of course there are the charla-tans who use smoke and mirrors, entertainers who trick the unwary. These frauds are useful, however, in obscuring the reality that there are real supernatural occurrences.)

My angels are also powerful. The orishas, gods and god-desses, even fairies, elves, and animal familiars will guide you through my realm of marvels and miracles. You may pre-fer the dark and steamy jungle origins of the Yoruba religion now expressed throughout the world as Santeria in Puerto Rico, Candomble and Macumba in Brazil, Voudon in Haiti, or Lucumi in Cuba. Or you may be attracted to the white, Northern European, pagan forms of my religions. How mys-terious and spiritually deep are the blends of what Druids, Celts, and Vikings have bequeathed to modern Wiccans.

These are just a few of my favorite kinds of worship. I am so pleased at the progress!

Miracles? Power? Yes, it is all real and available to you. You simply need to draw near to Me and my realm, submit to my rites and rituals, become an initiate of the dark arts, and adhere to one of many forms of my religions. Then I will have entry into your very being, to indwell you and give you my power, my miraculous gifts. How could you resist? You might not even know I was there, but the incredible exhilaration of supremacy will be yours to wield and enjoy!

• •

A Christian's response

The Devil's power cannot be denied. Jesus affirmed it. In Matthew 24:24 Jesus warned that false christs and prophets would be able to perform signs and wonders. These mirac-ulous displays would deceive many except those who were the elect, that is, genuinely converted people to Christ.

Paul warned about the power of evil in much the same way as Jesus did. In 2 Thessalonians 2:9-10, writing about events that would occur sometime in the future, he said, "The coming of the lawless one is by the activity of Satan with all power and false signs and wonders, and with all wicked deception for those who are perishing, because they refused to love the truth and so be saved." The so-called miracles fueled by Satan will be false signs, because they will not point to Jesus. The powerful and supernatural activities will successfully snare the unwary.

Some assume that anything miraculous must be from God. This assumption is error. Receiving a healing through occult practices, hearing the voice of a dead loved one, or having a fortune teller or palm reader describe events of the past that no one could have known are examples of the deception. Satan can do these things and more.

The medium or psychic is not necessarily intent on defrauding a client; in fact, many of them consider their work to be the result of a divine gift. The santero who charges large sums to cast a spell for the benefit of the "buyer" really thinks he or she is providing a worthy service.

But do not be deceived. Satan will not deliver what he promises. When the Devil says he wants entree into your very being to indwell you, he is being deceptive and really means demonic possession of you. Only God's Holy Spirit indwells the believer, and it is not for the purpose of acquiring power over the world or other people. It is for the power to be an effective witness for Jesus.

Trading one's personal autonomy, sometimes called "selling one's soul to the Devil," for temporary goodies like power, authority, fame, wealth, and psychic experiences only means that the Devil has you where he wants you, which is completely under his control.

This chapter causes me to wonder how close I came to being caught in the Devil's net during the period before I was born anew. I dabbled in UFOs, spiritualism, Edgar Cayce, Bridie Murphy, and other weird stuff, and somehow I escaped unharmed. In my research into Shamanism, Santeria, Wicca, Charisma, and more, I continually came across stories of people who directly encountered that which was spiritual, entities like dead ancestors, angels, gods and goddesses, animal guides, spirit guides, and so on, and they were absolutely taken over by it. Here was something undeniably real and spiritual. If that had happened to me, I might easily have been seduced.

One of the reasons Jesus appeared was to "destroy the works of the Devil."[2] In addition, Jesus gave his disciples power and authority over the demons of Satan.[3]

Jesus did not fear the Devil and his angels, and neither do those who trust in Christ as Lord. Even the psychics and practitioners of Santeria and other demonically-based religions know that Jesus Christ of Nazareth can cast out the demons that are possessing them. Nothing or no one else can, because Jesus alone is King of kings and Lord of lords.

---

2   See 1 John 3:8.

3   See Matthew 10:1 and Luke 9:1, 10:17-20.

Chapter 17:
Be Spiritual Not Religious

Strive to be spiritual, not religious. Value true spirituality, but abhor organized religion and its trappings. Those who live in the moment learn that spirit pervades the All, the Universe, which is my abode.

The Devil's Commentary

True spirituality is free. True spirituality rejects organized religion, which is just a for-profit institution. It is big business run by powerful, authoritarian men who misuse and abuse the trust accorded them. Their only interest is to have the poor, duped fools in the pews do their bidding, give money to their large church denominations and supposed "ministries," and basically take advantage of every opportunity to exploit those who are ignorant enough to submit to them. The fools who obey them must adhere to all the rituals, forms, and liturgy, say those ridiculous prayers over and over, light candles and incense, and give tithes! So much effort for what? I say it's all to enrich the fat-cats at the top.

All you have to do is look at the history of the megalomaniacal, so-called "Church," and you will see that I am speaking the truth. How many of the leaders of YKW's church preach saintliness from the pulpit but live lives of depravity and self-indulgence? Hypocrites!

• •
A Christian's response

If one is not religious, then one is not serious, since being religious is nothing more than incorporating one's faith into all of one's life.[1] A truly spiritual person will be religious by virtue of seeking and revering the sacred. Someone who jumps on every cool spiritual fad floating by may be little more than a dilettante, someone who is motivated by vain impulses.

The Devil says that religious people who are identified with organized denominations and churches are under suspicion of being phonies. Disturbing stories do hit the press from time to time, and some of the scorn is well-deserved. But the Devil's slamming of religious people is nothing more than an attempt to attack the message by attacking the messengers.

The Devil is also playing on the idealistic notion that if you are religious then you should be perfect or close to it. If a religious leader gets caught in bad behavior or does something considered stupid, then ipso facto, their whole belief system must be false and should be rejected. If, however, the same thinking were applied to other groups, then every imaginable institution or profession would be tainted at least. Do we condemn the entire fields they represent when we uncover corrupted judges, lawyers, police, doctors, dentists, teachers, politicians, CEOs, merchants, and so on? If one or more of these prove to be less than what they should be, must the whole bunch be considered unworthy or worse?

Again, the distinction between the visible and invisible church is vital. Anyone can be part of or join the visible church, which is comprised of groups and denominations. My family members are Baptists, but we can attest to the

---

1   The word "religious" comes from a Latin root that means "respect for what is sacred."

fact that not all Baptists are born-again Christians. Any Baptist pastor would likely agree with me. The same goes for any and all named and recognized Christian groups. It should not be shocking when ungodly behaviors occur in the name of God, from the medieval inquisitions to the financial and sexual scandals of church leaders that pop up all too often in today's headlines. The visible church is much like any institution – legal, political, medical, or financial. They are populated by sinful people in need of salvation. However, the invisible church is made up of those who are truly born again and known only to God. It is much smaller than the visible church.

Spiritual as opposed to religious? There is a significant distortion apparent here. By a vague contemporary definition, spiritual could be anything – meditating on the golf course, painting desert landscapes in New Mexico, casting a spell in a Wicca coven, fly-fishing in Oregon, surfing Hawaii's north shore, smoking some Maui Wowi, or banging on a war drum in a Native American sweat lodge. The implied understanding is that "natural" is closely related to spiritual, so the nearer one is to the unfettered original state of humanity before the influence of civilized society, the closer you are to being spiritual. The notion is that you can be natural and spiritual while avoiding the supposed trappings of "organized religion."

But are these things really spiritual? What is truly spiritual is the Holy Spirit of God, who always and only testifies of Jesus, both in terms of who He is and what He did. It is the Spirit who convicts us of our need of a Savior and reveals Jesus, the One who took our sin upon Himself on the cross, shedding His blood, dying, being buried, and then being raised from the dead. *That* is spiritual.

The people who lived in ancient Corinth, during the first Christian century, were very spiritual people. Paul said this to them: "The natural person does not accept the things of the Spirit of God, for they are folly to him, and he is not able to understand them because they are spiritually discerned."[2] The fact is, a person can be natural and spiritual in a worldly sense but not understand anything about God. The Corinthians Paul was addressing were indeed "religious," but they worshiped all sorts of idols and mythical gods and goddesses.

True spirituality and religiosity are one and the same. When Christ touches your life, forgives your sin, and gives you the gift of eternal life you *will* be serious, spiritual, and religious.

---

2   1 Corinthians 2:14.

Chapter 18:
Thou Shalt Not Believe in
J...s of Nazareth

*H**ere is the greatest commandment: Thou shalt not be-**lieve in J---s of Nazareth, and never refer to this hybrid creature as Lord J---s C----t. He is merely another teacher, of which there are a myriad. Acknowledge the existence of YKW, if you must, but the liberated ones let it go at that.*

The Devil's Commentary

My gospel is one of inclusiveness. We shun the "atheist" label and give lip service to the existence of YKW, but it's best to keep his identity as vague as possible. You can see that I am tolerant and generous. Yes, some of my best disciples will reason that if they believe in Me then why not my counterpart (among others).

What is a god anyway? I am the best of them. I am the god who rescues people from the restraining influences of YKW. I set them free to follow their basic instincts; I am the god of the people who know better.

The real problem is that person J...s, so if you must speak of him, at least make it part of your free speech right to swear and utter profanity to your heart's content. For your own comfort, stay away from the evangelicals who are constantly talking about Lord J...s this and that. If you see a cross on a church building or anywhere, or if you hear the name of the supposed offspring of YKW, shut your eyes and ears and head for the nearest exit.

Remember always this greatest of commandments: Thou shalt not believe in J---s. Amen and let it be.

• •

A Christian's response

The Devil has it right, so to speak: Jesus is the "real problem." He is indeed the center of it all. Jesus is God in the flesh, the only way to the Father. "Acknowledge the existence of" is not faith and does not foster worship. To believe and trust in Jesus is to believe in the Creator God. Satan will tolerate belief and worship of any god except the God and Father of the Lord Jesus Christ.

In that title, "Lord Jesus Christ," is the core message. "Lord" refers to His deity, that He is to be worshipped and honored, such as is due to God alone. He is to be obeyed and followed. "Jesus" is a form of the name Joshua and means "Yahweh Saves" or "Yahweh is Savior." In the Old Testament, Joshua was Moses' second-in-command when Israel escaped from captivity in Egypt. Moses led the nation through the wilderness, but Joshua led them into the promised land of Canaan. God equipped Joshua to finish His work of deliverance. "Christ" is another title that describes who Jesus is: He is the promised Messiah who saves His people and gives them rest. Christ is the Anointed One of God who was sent to redeem His people.

Therefore, it is not hard to understand why Satan must divert people from Jesus and toward literally anything else.

There is something else interesting here. It is the avoidance of anything, especially the cross, that would remind someone of Jesus. Many people who are under Satan's influence (whether they know it or not) cringe when a church, a cross, or a Bible are visually evident. Many Christians reacted just that way before their conversions, and it was completely unconscious. How this need to avoid all things Christian works I am not sure, but that it is an operative plan of attack,

I have no doubt.

I am reminded of Holy Redeemer Church in N.E. Portland, Oregon. My childhood friend, David Clark, was Catholic and went to that church. My problem was that it was right on the way to Peninsula Park where my brothers and I spent most of our summer days. I would walk on the other side of the street to avoid seeing it. David would invite us to come with him to church but I never accepted. Why this reaction? I have no idea, but now I am suspicious of where that revulsion came from.

The name of Jesus, spoken not in anger or carelessness, has an undeniable impact. No other name, whether spoken or in print, has such power. This is why the Devil wants us to utter it as an expletive - vainly, carelessly, and often - so as to sap it of its power. The name of Jesus retains its ability to stir up both love and loathing. Its impact cannot be denied.

Chapter 19:
Who Can Believe in a Virgin Birth?

The claim that a god had sex with a human, Mary, and of such a union a child was born, who was also called a god, is unbelievable and blasphemy of the worst sort!

The Devil's Commentary

YKW's book definitely says that his son was born like a human and that the mother was an unmarried virgin. Christianity is a perverse religion, with gods having sexual intercourse with creatures. That is disgusting. Enough said.

• •

A Christian's response

The Devil is assuming that terms in Scripture like *Son of God* and *Son of Man* will be misinterpreted. Indeed, the concept of God having sexual relations with His creation would be scandalous.

The term "son of man," which Jesus used to refer to Himself, goes back to the prophet Daniel, some hundreds of years before Jesus' earthly ministry. Daniel had a vision in which the term "son of man" occurs. Reading the account of the vision, it becomes clear why the term became a messianic title:

> I saw in the night visions, and behold, with the clouds of heaven, there ame one like a son of man, and he came to the Ancient of Days and was presented before him. And to him

was given dominion and glory and a kingdom, that all peoples, nations, and languages should serve him; his dominion is an everlating dominion, which shall not pass away. And his kingdom one that shall not be destroyed (Daniel 7:13-14).

Considering the authority and high praise given to the subject of Daniel's vision, it is no wonder that Jewish scholars recognized Daniel's "son of man" as a reference to the Messiah. Jesus adopted the term in speaking of Himself in order to connect to Daniel's prophecy.

Human language has its limitations. God's task of communicating Himself to us, who are severely limited in our ability to comprehend His ways, presents a challenge. He spoke through the prophet to describe the deity of the coming Messiah, not just that He would be a human being. That my son is human like I am human is obvious. In the same metaphorical way, the Son of God is divine like the Father. It has nothing to do with God-human sexual relations.

"Son of God" refers to the deity of Jesus: He is of the same being and essence as the Father, and "son of man" carries the same meaning. Both of these terms are used to designate the promised and prophesied Messiah of Israel.

Jesus was born of Mary, a virgin.[1] His birth fulfilled the prophecy foretold by Isaiah about the coming of the Messiah: "Therefore the Lord himself will give you a sign. Behold, the virgin shall conceive and bear a son, and shall call his name Immanuel."[2]

The virgin birth was a sign of the power of God. A human being, a son, would be born to the virgin, and the child's

---

1   *Almah,* in Hebrew means an unmarried young woman presumed to be virginal. To translate the Hebrew term in any other way than virgin would be to miss the "sign."

2   See Isaiah 7:14.

name would be called Immanuel, which means "God is with us." Here is the great mystery of the Christian Faith: God becomes human, all the while remaining God. We refer to Jesus as the God-Man. He is perfectly God and perfectly man simultaneously. How this could occur is a mystery that the Scripture makes no attempt to clear up, and no human being has been able to do so either.

Why must God become human? The answer is startling: so that He could die. The whole issue has to do with sin. Sin must result in death, which is more than physical death but includes eternal death, a separation from God forever. This is why there is a hell, that place where Satan will spend eternity. The Bible says that the wages, or outcome, of sin is death.[3] God in Christ died in the place of, or instead of, the sinner. But a sinner cannot die in place of other sinners. The sacrifice must be perfect. Only God is perfect; therefore, only God can die as a sacrifice. If you can understand this, then you have a grasp of the core doctrine of Christianity.

Immanuel – God had to become "with us," and He did when He was born of the virgin Mary in Bethlehem. She remained a virgin at conception, because this was accomplished by the Creator of all of life, God Himself. Even Mary did not understand how it could be. In answer to her confusion, the angel of God said to her, "The Holy Spirit will come upon you, and the power of the Most High will overshadow you; therefore the child to be born will be called holy – the Son of God."[4]

The name Jesus points to what He does. "Jesus" means "Yahweh saves" or "God is Savior" and was a common name for Jewish males during the first century A.D. Immanuel signifies who Jesus is. He is the One who has come to be with us. "The person and work of Jesus Christ" is how Christians refer to this.

---

3   See Romans 6:23.

4   Luke 1:35.

As an aside, the presence and work of the Triune God is evident in the birth of Immanuel. God the Father, God the Son, and God the Holy Spirit are one God, an *echad* (Heb.), a unity made up of three,[5] which then conforms to the constrictions of Deuteronomy 6:4, known as the *Shema* (Heb.): "Hear, O Israel, the Lord our God, the Lord is One." All three – Father, Son, and Holy Spirit – are deity in completeness. They are of the same essence, being, will, and intention.

---

5   A married man and woman are considered to be one, an echad, a unit, as we see in Genesis 2:24. "Therefore a man shall leave his father and his mother and hold fast to his wife, and they shall become **one** flesh."

Chapter 20:
You're Too Bad to be Forgiven

Bad is not evil; bad is better than trying to keep the impossible proscriptions of those goody types. Bad is real living, because even YKW says "all have sinned." Since we're all in the same boat, there's no sense in rowing to an illusory safety. Since it's too late to be anything but bad, just enjoy the party.

The Devil's Commentary

There are consequences, or so says YKW. So what? If you're gonna dance, you gotta pay the band. You expected something else? You've crossed the line, and now you're doomed forever to be the unforgiven. When you have been bad even once, it is over for you; therefore, you might as well give up trying to ever please YKW.

We bad ones didn't get that way by worrying. We are tough and can face anything. We want to have fun and get down and dirty, and we're not shy about it. If you've chosen bad, done really awful and disgusting things, then you know it's too late. If you have blasphemed to the extreme as I have, then you know you are unforgiveable, and you can't go back.

As for those of you who suffer guilt from doing bad and would rather choose good, quit whining and get over it. Even YKW's "teacher's pet," Paul, admitted he couldn't help doing what he hated. You think you're better than him?

You may as well worship Me openly, because I'm your only

hope now for finding friends and opportunities to use your "badness."

• •

A Christian's response

The Devil's strategy here is simple enough; attempt to convince people that they have offended God to such an extreme degree that they are utterly hopeless. Satan is the hopeless one, but no living human being is beyond hope.

Years ago a young woman showed up at our ministry house and was not able to communicate. It looked like catatonic schizophrenia to me. For hours she was mute and expressionless, so depressed she seemed frozen. Not knowing what to do, I simply seated her in a comfortable chair, got her some water, and let her be. Several hours later she began to mumble very quietly, and I took a seat nearby. Gradually she opened up. Her story was one I had heard before.

She had gotten involved in a witches' coven, both men and women participants, and after some brief period she had undergone an initiation. That initiation was so gross that I cannot relate it here, but it was designed to make her feel that she was so very awful and twisted that she could never be forgiven. When the initiation neared its conclusion, she was required to vow that she had given herself to Satan completely and totally. During the very last part of the rite she was made to repeat a long stream of profanities against the God of the Bible while urinating on a crucifix.

Bad she had been, but worse was that she believed what the witches told her, that she was no good at all and beyond redemption. It was my pleasure to tell her that those were all lies, and however bad she had been, the blood of Jesus Christ could cleanse away the most stubborn of stains. The Devil owns no one, regardless of any deal or soul-selling. I was so happy to point her to passage after passage in the Bible where Satan has been defeated and grace to forgive is abundant.

One of Jesus' parables broke the dam for her. It was the story of the Pharisee and the tax collector. The tax collector was a Jew who worked for the hated Romans and made a living by charging exorbitant rates beyond the tax that was called for. Here was a truly despicable traitor, but he still went up to the temple to pray.

At the same time a Pharisee went to the temple to do the same. He was part of a group who were highly esteemed by the populace for their piety and righteousness. The Pharisee was proud of the good deeds he routinely did, and while he was praying he mentioned the tax collector who was standing nearby. The religious leader boasted about how much better he was than that miserable wretch.

The tax collector did not look up to heaven, as was the custom when praying, but rather beat on his chest as a sign of desperation and said, "God be merciful to me, a sinner."

The conclusion to the parable was dramatic. Jesus said that the tax collector went out of the temple justified rather than the Pharisee. *Justified.* Jesus meant that the hated tax collector was completely forgiven of his sin.[1]

Being justified is not dependent on anything a person can do and has nothing to do with what has happened in the past. It is all about the mercy of God who simply loves to bring back to Himself those who think they are hopeless.

Satan does not want this fact to be known. He wants "bad" people to think they have been so very bad that they are beyond hope. This is nothing more than a complete lie. That young woman who thought she was beyond hope due to her experience in the witch's coven felt the forgiving mercy of Christ and became a strong Christian.

---

1   Find the parable at Luke 18:9-14.

Chapter 21:
"Good" and "Evil"
are False Concepts

You were created good, and thus you do good. Did not YKW say that all of His creation was good?[1] There is no good versus evil. It's all good. We are not evil but good, and we must reject those who restrain the pursuit of our natural goodness.

The Devil's Commentary

You would never have thought in terms of evil without that arbitrary list of commandments. How can it be good to create people, then restrict their behavior, casting the transgressor of even one tiny rule into hell forever? It makes Me suspicious that what is called "good" is really evil. One command was given, or so the story goes (if you can believe it), and YKW's original people didn't stand a chance. They naturally broke that one single little command.[2] Who would concoct such trickery? It might as well have been a trap set for a dumb animal. Why didn't YKW create a creature who could not err?

The concepts of good and evil are human constructs, so who is to say what is right or wrong? You are basically a good person, and you know it. So pursue your own good.

---

1 See Genesis 1:31.

2 See Genesis chapters 1-3.

• •

A Christian's response

The original human beings were created good, which is true enough. However, they broke the only commandment given to them. They were forbidden to eat the fruit of the Tree of the Knowledge of Good and Evil, but they succumbed to temptation and failed.[3] The breaking of that one commandment in the Garden of Eden was the seminal event that launched the Devil's relentless pursuit of human destruction. It is not surprising that he would address the subject again, since it is the foundation of all that went wrong in human history.

The existence of good and evil is a reality in our world, not an invention. In a way no one fully understands, knowing what is evil motivates us to do evil. At the first instance of this, trouble entered the world, and the result was lost fellowship with our Creator and the unbearable burden of sin. For our protection (mainly from ourselves), laws delineating good and evil were generated by God and subsequently by humans as well. Whole systems of law have developed, and if they were not in place, evil would reign and life would be vile and chaotic.

Can we do good? Yes and No is the answer, because there are differing opinions here. Yes, we can do good things, at least from the human perspective. We can give to the poor and be compassionate and kind, but true altruism, which is selfless acts with only the benefit of others in mind, is at best extremely rare. That is my evaluation of the human condition. I would not presume upon God's view of it.

No matter how good and obedient we might be, there is no value in struggling to earn God's favor. The pagan gods and goddesses could appear to be influenced by sacrifices and submission, but not the Holy God of Israel. He cannot

___
3   See Genesis 2:15-17.

be bribed. Ultimately, reconciliation between Almighty God and man only comes through one thing, and that is the atonement for sin through the shed blood of Jesus Christ. Only that perfect sacrifice can make us right with God.

Before the Law of Moses was given at Sinai,[4] sin was less restrained; evil prevailed. That is the story of Noah and his times. "The LORD saw that the wickedness of man was great in the earth, and that every intention of the thoughts of his heart was only evil continually."[5] Has anything changed?

In one of the most vivid and striking historical dramatic prophecies ever, God sent torrents of rain, and only Noah and his immediate family survived in the ark. The destruction of the flood was actually a gracious act of God; otherwise, the people would have destroyed themselves. The Law came next. Restraint was necessary, without which evil would rule through those with the most power. Enforcement of the Law was in the control of humans and was therefore flawed.

The Devil applauds the casting off of restraint; the Devil hates law and loves anarchy. Pursuing pleasure for pleasure's sake creates addiction and misery. We know this now. If the Devil could, and he is hard at it, he would ban laws that place limits on all manner of errant or heinous human activity. He would start with discarding laws dealing with sexuality, such as the age of sexual consent, plural marriage, same-sex marriage, bestiality, and more. He would campaign to eliminate laws against child abuse, spousal abuse, and elder abuse. Also on his list for removal would be laws against slavery, human trafficking, medical euthanasia, and assisted suicide. He would have people who object to his measures declared law-breakers. Satan would even like to make it illegal to *think* contrary to his unrestrained ways.

There will come a time, toward the end of history as we know it, when restraint will be removed. In the Bible it is

---

4   See Exodus 20.

5   Genesis 6:5.

called "the rebellion." Due to its great importance, the entire passage bears quoting:

> ³ Let no one deceive you in any way. For that day will not come, unless the rebellion comes first, and the man of lawlessness is revealed, the son of destruction, ⁴ who opposes and exalts himself against every so-called god or object of worship, so that he takes his seat in the temple of God, proclaiming himself to be God. ⁵ Do you not remember that when I was still with you I told you these things? ⁶ And you know what is restraining him now so that he may be revealed in his time. ⁷ For the mystery of lawlessness is already at work. Only he who now restrains it will do so until he is out of the way. ⁸ And then the lawless one will be revealed, whom the Lord Jesus will kill with the breath of his mouth and bring to nothing by the appearance of his coming. ⁹ The coming of the lawless one is by the activity of Satan with all power and false signs and wonders, ¹⁰ and with all wicked deception for those who are perishing, because they refused to love the truth and so be saved. ¹¹ Therefore God sends them a strong delusion, so that they may believe what is false, ¹² in order that all may be condemned who did not believe the truth but had pleasure in unrighteousness.⁶

What restrains Satan now is unknown. Perhaps it is the Church, or the Holy Spirit, or simply the plan of God – but in any case, the Devil is lawless and wants to throw off restraint.

Notice what awaits the Devil. If he reads God's Bible, he is well aware of his fate, whether or not he believes it. Jesus, the conquering champion of God, will defeat the Devil and

---

6   2 Thessalonians 2:3-12

his entire demonic kingdom once and for all. Satan intensely wields his wicked deception, using false signs and wonders in an attempt to turn truth on its head and convince anyone and everyone that good is bad and bad is good, while paradoxically preaching that there is no such thing as good or evil.

Experience reveals that there is good and evil. It is intuitive; we know it in our inner being. The Devil has to pull out all the stops to convince us otherwise.

Chapter 22:
Gain Strength from Division
Not Unity

Division is more powerful than unity. Unity, supposedly the result of loving and serving, is what the weak must rely upon. For the strong and independent, unity is a false ideal. The rule above all others is, "Do unto others before they undo you."

The Devil's Commentary

Love – what does that mean anyway? No one really knows, and no one gets it right, so be done with it. Rugged individualism is the ideal. Isolate, separate, and fulfill your own destiny. Help others only if it advances your own agenda; otherwise, don't waste your time.

The followers of YKW have their churches, but they are forever fighting with each other. All their talk about unity is pure jargon. They are constantly dividing and arguing. How many denominations are there? Hundreds, thousands, more? Who knows, as it keeps getting worse. The son of YKW was so ignorant that he said people would be very impressed by his followers' love for one another. That certainly did not come to pass. (That was just one of many predictions he got wrong. Not much of a prophet, was he?)

My commandments work in real life. My own do not have to waste their effort pretending to care for each other. I say, be your own person.

• •

A Christian's response

Jesus did tell us to love one another; He even said that such love would be evidence that we were truly His disciples. And it must be confessed that such loving and caring for each other in the Body of Christ has not been regularly accomplished. But it is there in ways that may not be evident to everyone.

True Christians will have arguments about things both minor and major, and those disagreements can be healthy. We come from a multitude of countries, cultures, and ethnicities. We speak most of the world's languages and have differences in politics, economics, and social agendas. Yet we need not be overly concerned about unanimity in these spheres; our true unity is in Christ.

Christians are indeed commanded by Jesus to love one another, to serve one another, and to treat others as they would want to be treated. Though we fail at meeting these high standards, it is better to have them as ideals than not. At least we have them as a measure of our behavior and a direction to guide us forward.

Sinful self-centeredness is common to our rebellious nature. Of course the Devil preaches a narcissistic message, because his own power is what he aims for, and seeking unity with others detracts from that goal. A person who is alone and self-focused is a person who is ripe for a takeover. "Divide and conquer" is a maxim most of us have heard many times. The Devil's ability to divide us leads to his ability to conquer us.

Chapter 23:
"Saints" are Boring Do-gooders

Lucifer is my name – Bright Star am I. Brilliance and light have been poured into my being, making for the ultimate in excitement and interest. I Am Me and ever will be. It will be said of my chosen ones that they lived extreme lives full of intensity and daring. This cannot be said of the boring, so-called "saints" of YKW's book.

The Devil's Commentary

Consider the accounts of the ordinary, commonplace characters recorded in YKW's book. Maybe a few of them do something dangerous or "important" by YKW's standards, but they pay a high price for their obedience. Their lives are over-burdened or destroyed trying to meet the demands put on them. Take Noah, who plods along for decades to satisfy YKW's demand for a huge boat. He never gets to engage in the exciting culture around him. If YKW were so all-powerful, he would provide the boat himself by some kind of magic. Instead, Noah suffers through horrible drudgery and ridicule.

In YKW's book all the characters are so "saintly" and "good," which makes for really boring reading. Who wants to emulate angelic types playing harps on clouds?

Is this the kind of life my own are called to? No, my commandment is to stretch to the breaking point every rule and restriction the rigid-minded religionists would foist upon you. Avoid drudgery in the name of spirituality!

The real reason those characters in YKW's bible are so boring is because the stories about them have been sanitized. I know for a fact that plenty of very interesting material was simply left out. How do I know? I was there, tempting, enticing, inciting, and working on them full time. They and those who wrote about them all attempted to hide what sorry losers they really were. Why does YKW try to fool everyone anyway? If he were really interested in telling the truth, he would disclose what those "saints" were really like. They were ordinary clods like most everyone else who doesn't follow my way.

• •

A Christian's response

Lucifer, bright but rebellious, was once cast away from that which is truly Light and became darker than the absence of light. This same Prince of Darkness will be chained forever in the deepest darkness. He urges us to seek "extreme lives" full of "ultimate excitement." The Devil may want people to think that lives of moderation are extremely boring, but those who go the Devil's way will only experience eternal boredom with their dreadful lot. There is nothing to boast of here.

Sin is boring: living for yourself is totally boring, unfulfilling, unsatisfying, and completely empty. The Devil hopes to make it look like those who obey his commands are the "real" people. They are not any more real than anyone else, but they are duped, blinded, and deceived by the master of lies himself. It is no great achievement to be defrauded by the biggest scam artist on the planet.

Let me clear up one point. "Saint" means set apart or called out; it does not mean without sin or perfect. Cartoonists draw images of saints wearing long white robes and sitting on clouds playing harps. A saint is a sinner saved by grace, and not saved because they were good but because they were sinners and knew it.

Consider Moses. Though a Jew, he grew up in the Egyptian king's household. When he finally asserted himself at age forty and checked on the plight of his kin who had been made slaves, he ended up killing an Egyptian overseer, tried to cover up the murder, fled when discovered, and stayed away for forty more years. He met God, was instrumental in major miracles that brought the most powerful nation of his time to its knees, and spent his last forty years leading millions of Hebrews through the desert. As we see Moses' story unfold in the Book of Exodus, we see that he had some high and low experiences.[1] Any way one looks at it, his is not the biography of a boring or unblemished life.

Consider David, anointed by God to be king. Although a married man, David watched the married Bathsheba taking a bath. He lusted after her, seduced her, then to cover his tracks when he found out his affair resulted in a pregnancy, conspired to murder her husband. Then he continued to lie about it until a prophet of God exposed him. What a life David lived! He was a sinner, yet God used him mightily.[2]

Consider Peter, "saintly" Peter. When Jesus called him, Peter's response was, "Depart from me, for I am a sinful man."[3] Perhaps you've heard the story: Peter denied Jesus three times and shortly after that tried to kill a member of the squad who came out to arrest Jesus.[4] Later there was trouble between Paul and Peter, and it is clear in the biblical account that Peter was in error about a very key doctrine.[5] Peter was far from perfect, both before and after he became a follower of Jesus. Yet he also was used mightily by God.

---

1   See Exodus chapter two and following.

2   See 2 Samuel 11 and following.

3   Luke 5:8.

4   See John 18:10.

5   See Galatians 2:11-14.

Consider Paul. A more zealous man for his Jewish religion would have been hard to find. He persecuted Christians and was responsible for having them killed. He did not spare women or children. He hated Jesus and those who believed in Him, but after his conversion all that changed. Paul became the greatest of Christian missionaries. Was he perfect? Not according to Paul himself. He had the humility and courage to confess that the things he did not want to do he did, and the things he wanted to do he did not do.[6] Often an odd man, Paul lived an authentic life, rich in challenge and adventure, but he was not a perfect human being by any standard.

There were others: Abraham, Isaac, Jacob, Samson, Solomon, and many more. They were real people whom God changed, and even when they fell flat on their faces, God lifted them up and caused them to stand. They left their ordinary and boring lives to serve the true and living God.

Followers of Jesus are real people called by God to mature into being like Christ. And this is not boring, far from it. It is rather the greatest challenge and adventure imaginable. Far more interesting to us than the deceptive plans of Satan are what God has in mind for His people. These words that God spoke to the prophet Jeremiah can be applied to His people today: "For I know the plans I have for you, declares the LORD, plans for welfare and not for evil, to give you a future and a hope."[7]

Now I consider myself, since I partially fell for this particular demonic lie, which labels saints as boring:

After moving from Portland, Oregon to Los Angeles in 1955, I became a wild kid by age fifteen, was even arrested for two felonies, and barely escaped doing real time in jail. I loved to steal and drink booze, and I liked gang fighting. I chased girls as hard as I could, and tried to emulate the

---

6   See Romans 7:7-28.

7   Jeremiah 29:11.

life style I read about in Jack Kerouac's book, *On the Road.* I was indeed a southern California surfer dude. When God waylaid and rescued me at age twenty-one, things radically changed.

My life has turned out to be anything but boring; in fact, I am hoping now for things to slow down some. Likely they will not, but at least I am enjoying nearly every minute.

Chapter 24:
"Saints" are Terrible Sinners

Consider the patriarchs who were so-called "faith heroes," whose lives are recounted in that other bible. Patriarchs like Moses, David, Paul, and all the rest were murderers, adulterers, deceivers, and liars. You can't expect to do "right" with such terrible "heroes" as examples. Those who follow YKW are following after the worst human models. My people live better lives than they do.

The Devil's Commentary

David was a "man after YKW's own heart," (whatever that means). So exactly who was this King David? I'll tell you. He was a murderer, adulterer, liar, and more. The whole sordid story is told in that other bible. How about David's parenting skills, did he have children who loved him? No. One of David's sons murdered another, and a third son rebelled against him, trying to take over the throne. What kind of example is he?

Saul was with Me for some time before he went his own way (and became Paul), claiming some kind of flashing-light conversion experience on that road to Damascus, but not before he did my bidding to the point of murder. And this is the person YKW chose to be a major leader and whose weird correspondences ended up in that other book! That was terrible judgment on YKW's part, choosing someone with such a soiled background to be a chief author for his book.

A Christian's response

It looks like the Devil wants it both ways. He rejects the "boring" and "saintly" biblical characters, but he also rejects the same people for being "terrible examples." He does not want you to know the power of God's Holy Spirit to change lives.

David and Paul were flawed people, sinful to the core. They were just like us, rebels against a holy God. And just like them we can be changed and converted in a moment. It's not that we believers suddenly become perfect. But we are made perfect in His sight.

It is a miracle that Christians are made perfect in God's sight. "Justified" is a word that is used to describe the complete transformation that occurs at the new birth. We are forgiven, even though we have done many bad things. All wrong-doing, every despicable act, no matter how evil and secret, is deleted and blotted out forever.

It takes us Christians some time before we realize that we have been placed "into" Jesus Christ and are now and always will remain free of guilt. How God accomplishes this defies the imagination, but the miracle is true nonetheless.

Christians are still sinners, but we grow steadily into the fullness of Jesus and learn to turn from and hate our sinful ways, just like the biblical heroes David and Paul. We do not boast in ourselves but in God alone and His grace that transforms us.

It is a huge paradox that the Christian is both a sinner and perfect at the same time. This mercy and grace is beyond us, but that does not negate its reality.

So why are the flawed, like David and Paul, recorded in Scripture? One reason is so we can see that no matter how crazy we are, the God who made us loves us still and will never turn away from us. What might seem to the Devil as a mistake or foolishness is in fact the wisdom of God.

Chapter 25:
Communicate with the Dead

*T*hose who know the secrets of the soul know that all the souls of the ages are yet present and may be contacted. Our beloved ones hover nearby, yearning for the chance to communicate with us, advise us, and comfort us to know they are still with us and are evolving into higher beings. Contact with these departed loved ones is best accomplished in the realm of Spiritism, my favorite spiritual philosophy and part of so many religions. My followers are never alone, since the spirits of those who have passed are waiting to speak – with you. Reach out and contact them now!

The Devil's Commentary

My truths are multi-dimensional and often appear to contradict one another. "The grave is the end," I have said. That is truth for those who believe it is truth. There is "other" truth for those who desire more subtlety and sophistication. As varied as people are, so are my doctrines. We must not be exclusive, hemmed in by narrow strictures and stand-alone concepts; YKW does this constantly, and it is very boring. One way, one truth? Only the simple-minded limit themselves so.

Therefore, as I always say, "The grave is *not* the end," because our dearly departed ones remain to serve our needs for comfort and encouragement, to bring us knowledge of the wonderful world beyond, and to help us to spiritual maturity.

You will gain an advantage in this dismal world of hard, cold reality, if you contact the spirits of the dead and learn as much from them as possible. Your own spirit will experience the exhilaration of hearing and seeing what really happens after death. Instead of simple-minded, choose open-minded and open-spirited.

• •

A Christian's response

The Devil does not seem to care that his doctrines are mutually exclusive. He does not care whether you believe that the grave is the end or that the dead remain to communicate with the living. He only cares that you believe something different from the truth of the Bible.

Spiritism is a belief system that explains phenomena via the general principle of the survival of a "spirit" or "soul" after death, called "evolutionary reincarnation" (only from human to human). In a stricter sense, Spiritism is a doctrine founded upon the existence, manifestations, and teachings of the "spirits." Spiritists believe that they can contact the dead through séances, the Ouija board, mediums, channellers, psychics, shamans, and so on. It may be comforting to some, but it is horrible error that can lead seekers down a dark road to unholy spiritual bondage.

For millennia, demons have been disguising themselves as the souls[1] of dead people. It is called necromancy in Deuteronomy 18:10-12. Those who style themselves as mediums supposedly contact the dead and relay messages. In séances, spirits of the dead seem to speak through the medium, possess the medium, and sometimes even materialize. Those who witness these things may embrace other demonic concepts as a result.

---

1   We do not have souls so much as we *are* soul. Soul indicates that humans are more than material, all the while having a spiritual aspect to our being, a built-in spirituality intended by the Creator.

Do the dead contact the living? Are the dead, including atheists and a wide variety of non-Christians, enjoying something other than the hell Scripture teaches? The medium gives the message from the contacted soul, "I am okay here," or words to that effect. Who would not be persuaded? The Devil wants nothing more than for people to think there are three primary possibilities after death. One, there is no life after death at all. Two, everyone lives on in spirit but not flesh. Three, souls will reincarnate to live on earth (or even on another planet) again.

When a person dies, Christian or not, that is the end of their contact with the world of the living on the planet. This we understand from the parable Jesus told about the rich man and Lazarus. An impassable chasm or barrier prevents any interaction between the living and the dead.[2]

The comfort that seems to be offered through contact with the dead is false comfort at best, and at worst it is a demonic lie that it is intended to prevent people from trusting in Jesus as Savior and Lord.

Yes, there is a spirit world, and the mediums and psychics are not necessarily tricksters and fakers. But what they think are the souls or spirits of the dead are nothing more than demons impersonating the dead. It is very deceptive and convincing, but devilry all the same.

At the heart of this deception is the trance state, passive state of mind, or altered state of consciousness. This is what religions like Shamanism, Santeria, and Wicca depend upon.[3] The trance is the means by which the souls of the dead and other spiritual entities are encountered. It is dramatic and life-changing to see this, and it easily moves a person from a materialist to a spiritist. However real it all seems, it is still a production enacted by demonic spirits.

---

2   See Luke 16:26.

3   Philpott's book, The "Soul Journey" Connection: Shamanism, Wicca, Santeria, and Charisma, is available at www.evpbooks.com.

Chapter 26:
Purify Your Soul
through Reincarnations

Your soul is immortal. That is clearly taught even by the church of YKW. After death, your soul must be reborn into another person. Each time you go around, you work out the issues and problems of your past lives. This is the method by which you purify your soul and become an ever higher being.

The Devil's Commentary

Immortality of the soul manifests itself through reincarnation. Even the church of YKW knows that. How else could it be that you have existed before the beginning of time, as YKW says? It is only logical that you were not waiting around for millions of years, just to be born one time only.

The truth is that you have been here many times before in previous bodies and personalities. That is how you have become so wise. Didn't I say that the grave is not the end? We have many opportunities to get life right and purify our souls. The smart ones have consulted mediums or other fine practitioners who understand the deeper, more mysterious things and have found out they lived many lifetimes before. This adds great depth and dimension to their current lives and gives them an advantage that others don't have.

Reincarnation is a wonderful method of purifying the soul and becoming better followers of Me. In this way, you will live forever, just like Me!

• •

A Christian's response

Reincarnation is the belief that the souls of the dead will inhabit a new body after the old body expires. The western-ized version states that a human being can be reincarnated only into a new human body.[1] Amazingly, Satan doesn't seem to care that this belief is contradictory to both the idea that the souls or spirits of the dead stay in some place of limbo awaiting the chance to communicate with the living and the idea that the grave is the end. All three are errors.

Belief in reincarnation is a favorite ploy of Satan, because it lulls adherents into believing that they have no need to deal with the consequences of sin in their lives and therefore have no need of a Savior. Other ploys, like an intermediate state of limbo or purgatory, are at best human inventions developed to soften the horrors of death and give false com-fort to the living. Scripture speaks nothing of these ideas. Instead it says, *"It is appointed for man to die once, and after that comes judgment."*[2] What better way to avoid the reality of that word "judgment" than to believe that you get many, perhaps even unlimited chances to "get it right," sometimes called "working out your karma." It sure removes the moral burden, doesn't it?

Judgment will indeed come, and it will be based on what we have done in our one lifetime here on earth. After that, we will, in fact, live forever, but not because of reincarnation. Rather, we live because of resurrection, the raising of the dead at the second coming of Christ. All will be raised, the

---

1   In the more original Hindu concept of reincarnation, the num-ber of reincarnations required to overcome bad karma are counted in the thousands. Westerners need something more palatable, so some "enlightened ones" teach that you can get it right in just one lifetime. Hmm – the Devil's advertising department is working overtime.

2   Hebrews 9:27.

just to eternal life and the unjust to eternal punishment.[3] It is this somber truth the Devil wants to obscure. The devil well knows that if a person sees reality, then he or she might have an interest in Jesus.

---

3   See Acts 24:15 and Matthew 25:46.

Chapter 27:
Enter a Higher Plane through
Meditation and Trance

Focus your mind and attention on my kingdom, and you will be at peace. Go to your sacred space, inside the circle or in front of your altar; then relax, center, balance, and ground yourself. Now breathe deeply, softly chanting my name, and your meditation will merge into a deep space, that blissful trance state where you will encounter Me and mine. Stress and anxiety will flee, your heart rate will drop, and the pleasure centers of your brain will sparkle.

The Devil's Commentary

My people do not need to pray. They need only meditate, empty their minds, get as close to nothingness as possible, and in that place encounter an ally, a friend, or a guide to advise and give comfort.

Praying is what YKW's people do. Their minds never turn off. They are always begging YKW for something - thinking, asking, pleading, and worrying. They pray to who knows what and who knows where. I, or rather, my agents, indwell my followers and make it easy to fall into a blissful state of mind, an altered state of consciousness, wherein your spirit-friends reside.

And how easy it is! After a time, my most adept disciples can go into their sacred space, their base camp as it were, almost at will, and find their guide waiting to take them on a journey to places of wonder.

There is a way into spiritual trance for everyone. Some meditate, others chant and meditate, some focus and meditate. Others get into that blissful state of mind through dance, or listening to drumming, or (this is my favorite of all) in many of YKW's own churches singing their endless, vapid churchy choruses, swaying to the beat of an overly loud band, with eyes closed and arms raised, slipping into states of consciousness wherein I have access to them. YKW may think I can't reach those inside the church building; wrong. There they think they're safe and let their guard down, making themselves vulnerable and available for spiritual houseguests.

· ·

A Christian's response

Christians pray and connect with their Lord. Not only is each follower of Jesus indwelt by the Holy Spirit, but each one also has access to the very presence of God through the atoning sacrifice of Jesus on the cross. Our heavenly Father is ready to hear the concerns of His sons and daughters.

Trance or altered states of consciousness are indeed realities, but they are states of mind wherein one becomes vulnerable to the deceptions of Satan and his demons. The guides, the spirits, or the allies are merely demons, though they disguise themselves as animals, elves, fairies, ancestors, and so on. It is, in fact, happening in the "spiritual" world and is not necessarily magic-act trickery or illusion. It is so real that people are often stunned and feel overwhelmed and shocked to actually encounter proof of a spirit world. (I have written of this in an earlier chapter, but it is such a large issue, I felt it needed to be emphasized again.)

As odd as it might seem, and it is strange even to biblically-literate Christians, Satan is a master masquerader. He is able to mimic or counterfeit the authentic charismatic gifts of the Holy Spirit, which include everything from healings to miracles of all sorts. Not everything supernatural is necessarily from God. The Devil is "spiritual," as are his demons, but they are *unclean* spiritual, not *holy* spiritual.

Sadly, in attempts to contextualize, in efforts to meet contemporary culture where it is, potentially dangerous forms of worship have crept into the Christian environment. Centuries ago there were so-called "Christian mystics" who attempted to achieve union with Christ in unbiblical ways and who crossed the line into occult practices using forms of meditation that were unbiblical. These unbiblical practices have persisted into our own day.

There are many effective ways to alter one's state of consciousness. Unfortunately, in many evangelical and pentecostal forms of Christianity is the creation of ambiances meant to be worshipful but which encourage altered states of consciousness similar to those found in decidedly non-Christian venues. The Devil is certainly capable of capturing these methods for his own purposes. The beat of the drum, the thumping of the base guitar, the droning on and on of choruses with words of praise that could be addressed to almost any god or goddess, the flashing of beautiful nature scenes, dimmed lights, bodies moving to the beat, large crowds swaying together and urged on by "worship" leaders. It is no wonder that some in these environments are being caught up in the moment and made vulnerable to dark forces.

Christians praise and worship, sing and dance, and lift up holy hands to God. But Christian worship is mindful, alert, and full of Bible content. Christians meditate, but it is focused on the words and work of God, all of which is derived directly from Scripture. For the Christian, the mind is not an enemy or an obstacle to spirituality that must be circumvented in order to "tap" into realms where spirit is contacted.

Christian worship may be corporate; Jesus said where two or more gather because of and in praise of Him, there

He is. Or it can be individual, since the Holy Spirit indwells the believer always, regardless of his or her state of mind or heart.

While worship of God may be joyful, and Christians may have emotional experiences, we do not speak of "feeling" the Holy Spirit. Christians *know* that God's Spirit is present with us as believers, but we do not ascribe moments of jubilation or happiness to be the prime evidence of the presence of the Holy Spirit. No matter what our mood is, in contentment or despair, in elation or distress, God is with us.

There are those who claim certain physical "benefits" from meditation techniques, thus hoping to justify the practice. Those who pray often claim the same health benefits that are allegedly obtained through meditation. But changes in brain chemistry and the lowering of blood pressure neither prove nor justify anything. Christians do not spend time in prayer and biblically-oriented meditation in order to receive health benefits; we do so to come before the God who loves us.

Chapter 28:
Imagine

Imagine no religion; it is easy if you try. No hell below us; above us only sky. It's even easier, if you believe in Me. Live for yourself every day. No need for more. Then all the people will be at peace.

The Devil's Commentary

The religious wars, the bigotry, and the rules would all be gone if the religions dissolved and became as One. The one great spiritual practice of deep meditation would then be universal. All would know the trance-producing spiritual practice where the mind is shut down and negated. All the world's peoples should practice this, though it takes discipline and guidance.

Open yourself to the possibilities abounding in the Universe. Imagine the wisdom of the ages, the sages able to guide and teach, and the powers, authorities, and principalities awaiting entrance into a cleared soul. The One Mind, which is *my* mind, *my* soul, *my* consciousness, is hovering and anticipating an invitation to come in and abide; and I will certainly do it. Open and abandon your mind and receive more than you can imagine.

• •

A Christian's response

Look beneath the surface of the Devil's so-called invitation to "come in and abide," which is language he borrows from

Jesus, who said, "Abide in me, and I in you. As the branch cannot bear fruit by itself, unless it abides in the vine, neither can you, unless you abide in me."[1] You can see the subtle way that the Devil imitates God but perverts it into a mechanism by which he takes possession of an individual. The unwary person does not realize what manner of "invitation" this is and what has happened to him or her. Clever indeed, but a distortion as usual.

However, we do not congratulate Satan, since his ultimate purpose is spiritual murder and eternal imprisonment. To the person who imagines he or she is opening up to the promised secrets of the universe, the reality is anything but fulfilling. An "enlightened one" wakes up in the darkness alone and hopeless, only to find it is too late.

Despite the lovely-sounding sentiments of a popular song, there is no escaping that the lyrics all fit neatly into the Devil's view of things. He, too, is fond of saying, "I hope someday you'll join us, and the world will live as one."

---

1   See John 15:1-11 and 1 John 2:24.

Chapter 29:
I Will Return in Power
and Authority

*F*ear not! That which has been hidden from the beginning of time is now revealed. I will be coming again in
power in the last days. My glory will be made manifest in
my Appointed One, my Antichrist. Finally I will be incarnate and walking among you.

The Devil's Commentary

For long millennia I have been hampered by YKW, yet I'm
not without power. But soon and very soon, great signs and
wonders will be performed by my Appointed One. Be watch-
ful, be alert, for he will suddenly appear, he and the very last
of the prophets. In my Chosen I will be amongst you, and
you will be my warriors, those favored ones who will carry
out my desires. It will be a glorious war!

Few know my power. It is only hinted at in that other bible.
I am the Prince of the Power of the Air and the God of This
World.[1] These are *my* titles, and they are even found in YKW's
book.

YKW sent that son of his to defeat Me.[2] I knew it was coming, because I listened as YKW told Adam and Eve way back
in the Garden of Eden that I would bruise her descendant

---

1   See Ephesians 2:2 and 2 Corinthian4:4.

2   See 1 John 3:8.

only in the heel, but he would bruise my head.[3] I admit that I only wounded him (J---s) when I arranged for that wonderfully enraged Jerusalem rabble to force the Romans to crucify him. I thought that would be the end of him, but no, he came back, and whatever he did on that cross stripped Me of my power.

Or so they think. The truth is I am alive and well on planet earth and in the entire universe, for that matter. Even though I am bound by chains[4], yet I walk among the peoples of the world through my emissaries, my messengers, my angels. I empower them and direct them; I am their Master. Through them I have gathered my own so that where I am they will be also. I will come for them, they will hear my voice, and follow Me to their appointed place.

The years of my tenure will be ending soon, but I will be about my business more powerfully than ever before. Be ready, for you never know when I will arrive.[5]

• •

A Christian's response

"Antichrist" he is called; Paul referred to him as "the man of lawlessness." Other names are the "son of perdition" and the "son of destruction." He operates by the power of Satan. "The coming of the lawless one is by the activity of Satan with all power and false signs and wonders."[6]

Jesus became incarnate but Satan cannot do the same. The best the Devil can do is possess a person who will be known as Antichrist because he will be against Christ and His elect.

The apostle John spoke of this Antichrist long ago and actually said that there were many antichrists already at

---

3   See Genesis 3:15.

4   See Revelation 20:1-6.

5   See Revelation 20:7-10.

6   2 Thessalonians 2:9.

work even during his day in the first century. "Children, it is the last hour, and as you have heard that antichrist is coming, so now many antichrists have come."[7] The last hour has been upon us since the days when Jesus walked on the earth. One of the reasons for the first coming (Advent) of the Messiah was "to destroy the works of the devil."[8] Satan was defeated at the cross and by Jesus Christ's resurrection and ascension. On that cross Jesus triumphed over Satan, death, and hell. He will finish the job at His second coming.

For reasons that are cloaked in mystery, Satan's chains will be loosed during the tribulation or time of trouble that is to come, and he will be able to wreak his havoc unfettered for one short, last time.[9] The Antichrist will appear, along with an even more mysterious person, the "False Prophet,"[10] and many will be deceived and join the Devil's rebellion against God and His people.

God's response to the great last battle is highly unusual, at least from a human perspective, but it fits into His ultimate intention. That response, which focuses on the plight of those who are deceived by Satan, is startling at minimum. Paul explained, "God sends then a strong delusion, so that they may believe what is false, in order that all may be con-

---

7   1 John 2:18.

8   See 1 John 3:8.

9   In Daniel 9, in what is known as apocalyptic language, the prophet speaks of Satan's rebellion in the last days of human history before the Second Advent of Jesus, which will last a short period of time, perhaps a few years. Since the days of the early Church, Christians have had a number of different ways of looking at this, and no one can be absolutely certain of all the details surrounding these events.

10   One viewpoint of the end times is that Satan is bound for 1,000 years, which may symbolically refer to the age of the Church, but at the end of that period he will be set free to deceive the nations of the world. Shortly thereafter, however, fire will come down from heaven, and the Devil will be thrown into hell along with the "Beast" or the Antichrist as well as the False Prophet. There they will be tormented forever. See Revelation chapter 20.

demned who did not believe the truth but had pleasure in unrighteousness."[11]

Those "who did not believe the truth but had pleasure in unrighteousness" willingly believe Satan's lies; thus, God seals the matter utterly by providing no avenue of return. This is a mystery and terrifying at the same time. It has to do with God's judgment, which the Devil never wants to bring up but which is certain.[12] All will stand before the judgment seat of God and be held accountable for their sins against Him. Those whose sins have been covered by the blood of Jesus will be seen by God as unblemished, washed white as snow. Those whose sins have not been forgiven will suffer the fate of Satan and his minions forever.

The Devil wants to populate his world – the abyss, hell, the lake of fire – with as many human beings as possible. This is his ultimate intention.

So the Devil wrote a bible. He wants followers. If his version of reality sounds exciting, it simply means you have already been deceived.

---

11   2 Thessalonians 2:12

12   See Revelation 20:10.

Not Commandments, Rather "Demonments"

Editor's note: The Devil now unveils his counterfeit version of what is called the "Ten Commandments." The original set is found in Exodus 20. As you will see, Satan writes his own version of the background events as well as his own list of commandments, which he calls demonments. The original scene as written by Moses is as follows:

> On the morning of the third day there were thunders and lightnings and a thick cloud on the mountain and a very loud trumpet blast, so that all the people in the camp trembled. Then Moses brought the people out of the camp to meet God, and they took their stand at the foot of the mountain. Now Mount Sinai was wrapped in smoke because the LORD had descended on it in fire. The smoke of it went up like the smoke of a kiln, and the whole mountain trembled greatly. And as the sound of the trumpet grew louder and louder, Moses spoke, and God answered him in thunder. (Exodus 19:16-19)

The Devil's revision is as follows:

> *Picture the scene: There they were, about 3,500 years ago, an unruly rabble called the Israelites. YKW had pulled some stunts he called miracles*

and badgered the poor, beleaguered Egyptians into letting perfectly contented, well-treated servants flee the country. Now that sorry old man Moses had them all huddled at the base of a mountain in the Sinai wilderness. They were hungry, tired, and cold and would do anything they were told in order to stay alive. As they cowered there in fear, YKW put on an intimidating light and sound show.

On the morning of the third day there were thunders and lightnings and a thick cloud on the mountain and a very loud trumpet blast, so that all the people in the camp trembled. Then Moses brought the people out of the camp to meet the Prince and Power of the Air – I AM ME - and they took their stand at the foot of the mountain. Now Mount Sinai was wrapped in smoke because the Great Lucifer had descended on it in fire. The smoke of it went up like the smoke of a kiln, and the whole mountain trembled greatly. And as the sound of the trumpet grew louder and louder, Moses spoke, and the Mighty Satan answered him in thunder.

Oh, such drama was wasted on YKW's version of this moment. Don't you just shutter with excitement at all my powerful names? Yet, instead of Me, the Jews got this Moses, a has-been murderer, an old geezer incapable of uttering two clear words. He was so disabled, he had to have his brother speak for him. Then Moses cooked up worn out clichés for laws that most of the Israelites could have cared less about. So, for the rest of their history they have been straight-jacketed into obeying overly strict, ridiculous mores or suffer execution right on the spot. And people think I am cruel!

Look at the commandments and you will realize that the vast majority of YKW's little saints have broken most, if not all, of them. The ten rules – that is what YKW is all about, rules and more rules – should be thrown out and replaced with contemporary suggestions. What I give you are suggestions and not authoritative, ego-centered commandments. After all, we should not live our lives trying to obey ridiculous rules intended for a bunch of Hebrew slaves who ran away from their rightful masters after abetting a horrific mass murder of innocent Egyptians. My followers will not be subjected to outdated laws and rules; my disciples will listen to Me, because I know what is best for them.

Demonment
ONE

(YKW's first commandment: "You shall have no other gods before me.")[1]

My first demonment: You shall be eclectic and worship whatever gods you wish.

The Devil's Commentary

AM I not a god? Indeed I AM! I AM the Master who will delight you with all that your mind and flesh crave. And do not ignore the other gods and goddesses, who are my high-placed officers. They can respond for your benefit,n when you make the proper offerings and sacrifices to them. Take advantage of all that my officers have to give. Have faith in many gods, worship and serve them in turn – but I will have the last say.

• •

A Christian's response

The Devil is a god, the "god of this world,"[2] and this designation is not one to be proud of. Demons, the fallen angels that sided with Satan, are quasi-gods, too. They do have power and gifts to give, and many people worship them, but those who do so do not realize they are actually *worshiping demons* and do not realize the terrible consequences

---

1   The Ten Commandments are found in Exodus 20:3-17.
2   See 2 Corinthians 4:4.

of those trade-offs until it is often too late.

God alone is the Creator; He spoke the universe into existence.[3] Therefore, He alone is worthy to be worshiped. Anything and everything else is idol worship, which is not only false and worthless but also dangerous.

The Bible clearly teaches that the gods, such as those worshiped by the nations surrounding Israel, have no objective reality,[4] even though their worshipers sincerely believe they actually exist.[5] But the Lord proclaims that "they are not really gods at all" and "are nothing" or are "beings that by nature are no gods."[6] Israel was warned about the dangers of following the worship practices of the peoples living around them as early as the time of the Exodus. They were told repeatedly throughout their history that the Lord is greater than all other gods.[7]

As God predicted, the people of ancient Israel were indeed tempted by their neighbors, so there is a reason that the very first commandment is, "You shall have no other gods before me." The great statement of faith of both Jews and Christians is, "Hear, O Israel: The LORD our God, the LORD is one."[8] Christians understand, based on Scriptural evidence, that God is a unity, a Three-in-One or One-in-Three, yet one God, one

---

3   See Genesis chapter 1. Several times during this story of creation we read, "And God said, 'Let there be...' followed by "And it was so."

4   Jeremiah 2:11: "Has a nation ever changed its gods (even though they are not really gods at all)? But my people have exchanged me, their glorious God, for a god that cannot help them at all!" Jer. 16:20: "Can man make for himself gods? Such are not gods!"(NET) Isaiah 41:23-24a: "Tell us what is to come hereafter, that we may know that you are gods;... Behold, you are nothing, and your work is less than nothing."

5   Jer. 2:28: "But where are your gods that you made for yourself? Let them arise, if they can save you, in your time of trouble; for as many as your cities are your gods, O Judah."

6   Galatians 4:8: "Formerly, when you did not know God, you were enslaved to those that by nature are not gods."

7   See Exodus 15:11; 18:11; Deut. 10:17; Joshua 22:22; 1 Chron. 16:25; 2 Chron. 2:5; Psalms 86:8; 136:2; Daniel 2:47; Zephaniah 2:11.

8   Deuteronomy 6:4

LORD, who alone should be worshiped. To worship God is to worship God the Father, the Son, and the Holy Spirit. As a unity, "the Father, the Son, and the Holy Spirit" is called the Holy Trinity.

"Christ in you, the hope of glory"[9] speaks to the grand miracle of the Holy Spirit of God indwelling the believer. The prophets of Israel looked forward to this.[10] Satan counterfeits this indwelling by invading, demonizing, or possessing those who worship him.

The Devil tells us to worship him instead of the One true God, although he does not require us to worship him directly. When we worship other gods or the idols that depict other gods, we worship the demons who lurk behind them, and it is the same as worshiping the Devil.

---

9   See Colossians 1:27.
10   See Jeremiah 31:31-34 and Ezekiel 37:14.

Demonment TWO

(YKW's second commandment:[1] "You shall not make for yourself a carved image, or any likeness of anything that is in heaven above, or that is in the earth beneath, or that is in the water under the earth. You shall not bow down to them or serve them, for I the LORD your God am a jealous God...")

My second demonment: You are free to create any image you want and worship it. I am not a jealous god.

The Devil's Commentary

The creative urge must be encouraged. And I am not jealous like YKW is. I say, make a representation of whatever you desire. Make it out of wood, stone, steel, mud, or dung. Let the artists among my disciples be free to express themselves. (Avoid those silly images of Me with the red suit, pitch fork, smoke coming out of the ears and so on, since that scares some folks and lacks imagination.) "Make grandiose art," is what I say. Think of the statue of the goddess Athena that sat in the Parthenon – what art, what beauty, so much to be worshiped.

YKW's book says that to worship an idol is to worship Me. No one believes that. YKW is just a jealous god who can't tolerate anyone bowing down to anything or anyone other than himself. I say he is egocentric or pathologically narcis-

---

1   A partial quote from the second commandment, Ex. 20:4-5a.

sistic at minimum. His second commandment should be rejected as squelching the creative spirit.

• •

A Christian's response

God as Creator gave humans an artistic impulse and the natural skills to make various forms of art. We see this demonstrated in the instructions for building the Tabernacle in the Book of Exodus and later in the magnificent Temple in Jerusalem, for which God gifted the builders and craftspeople with the skills needed to accomplish the job. The Temple was noted as one of the seven wonders of the ancient world.

Human creation of art is not the concern of the second commandment, rather it is the making of an image in order to worship it. That image or piece of art then becomes the god itself, even if it is only intended to prompt worship of the one whose image is depicted.

Scripture teaches that behind the idol is a demon. Serving idols (tangible images of gods and goddesses) is the same as serving and worshiping the Devil and the demons. Paul writes of this in 1 Corinthians 10:18-21:

> Consider the people of Israel: are not those who eat the sacrifices participants in the altar? What do I imply then? That food offered to idols is anything, or that an idol is anything? No, I imply that what pagans sacrifice they offer to demons and not to God. I do not want you to be participants with demons. You cannot drink the cup of the Lord and the cup of demons. You cannot partake of the table of the Lord and table of demons.

Two chapters earlier, in chapter 8 verses 5-6, the apostle tells why it is wrong to serve idols:

> For although there may be so-called gods in heaven or on earth – as indeed there are

many 'gods' and many 'lords' – yet for us there is one God, the Father, from whom are all things and for whom we exist, and one Lord, Jesus Christ, through whom are all things and through whom we exist.

The issue is that we are created by God, not by demons. We owe our being and our life to God, not to Satan.

Idolatry was rife in the ancient world, and a reasonable question is, have things changed much? Our idols may not be carved by famous artists, large pieces that decorate the agoras, stoas, and roadways of the ancient Greek and Roman cities, but we have our modern versions. Viewing television for a short while, flipping through pop publications, or surfing the internet will show that our idols are alive and well. These idols could be human beings, such as movie, TV, or sports stars; or possessions, property, and money; or our own physical bodies and their comfort and pleasure; or education or careers; or our spouses or children. The list can stretch to a great length, but the common ingredient is an inordinate admiration for and desire to have or to please something or someone other than the God of this universe. In other words, an idol is anything we prefer above Him. God's second commandment helps us ask, "to what are we giving ourselves?"

The idea that God is jealous is a frequent concept found in Scripture, and it means that God loves us so much, He would guard us from being won over by deception, just as a father jealously guards his child or a groom his bride.[2] He made us "in His image," which means He made us capable of relating to Him. He wants us to enjoy His presence forever. He does not want us to belong to Satan. It is good and right that God is "jealous" and cares for us, for if He were not jealous, He would not be a caring God.

---

2   See Exodus 34:14; Deuteronomy 4:24; 5:9; 6:15; Joshua 24:19; Ezekiel 36:6; Joel 2:18; Nahum 1:2; Zechariah 8:2.

Demonment
THREE

(YKW's third commandment: "You shall not take the name of the LORD your God in vain, for the LORD will not hold him guiltless who takes his name in vain.")

The third demonment: You are free to say whatever pleases you about anyone and everything, and profanity against YKW's name is encouraged.

The Devil's Commentary

I stand for free speech, so say and write what you will. Speak your mind and do it with gusto! If you get angry, let it be known with appropriate, spicy language. Do you really think YKW is recording everything you say and do? Impossible! Even I can't do that (though I am working on it). With Me you can do no wrong, especially when you take YKW's name in vain. If oath-taking pleases you, swear by *my* name. I love to hear my name on the lips of my disciples, particularly when they make appeals to Me and pledge to serve Me.

If you *have* sworn an un-pious oath using the name of YKW, then you are already guilty and may as well openly join my forces now. If you have lived to age twenty, you doubtless stand condemned. I rarely finish a sentence without breaking this third commandment, but in my case, what does it matter? Disregard YKW on this point and say what you will. Don't be dull and dreary like YKW's goody-goody followers.

Go ahead and drag his name through the mud. Use his name creatively in a curse. These are the sounds I love to hear.

• •

A Christian's response

The Devil, as usual, is not telling you the whole story. It is really much more nuanced than he lets on. "In vain" means to lie and cheat, all the while calling on the name of God or declaring an oath using the name of God. Or, it can refer to using names of God and other significant names referring to God in magical, occult formulas. So-called "white" or "neutral" magic, black magic, and undisguised Satan-worship will all employ formulas, oaths, and incantations that pilfer biblical names used to speak of the Father, Son, and Holy Spirit.

One book of magic that I examined on the occult had dozens of statements that seemed quite orthodox, but were being used to command, demand, or persuade an unholy deity into performing favors or actions on behalf of the demander. I found repeatedly throughout the occult book repetition of the Lord's Prayer and the Apostles' Creed, and other obviously Christian expressions. This is clearly an instance of taking the name of God in vain.

"Name" in Scripture is more than just a name; the name indicates the person. To take God's name in vain is to denigrate His holiness, justice, and love.

God revealed His name to Moses in Exodus chapter three. The Hebrew people considered that name to be so holy they would not pronounce it but rather used another word, transliterated *Adonai*, in place of the covenant name of God. The Hebrew letters for that holy name are YHWH, and that name is essentially unpronounceable and nearly indefinable. It means, variously, The One Who Is, The Being Infinite and Eternal, I Am Who I Am, I Am, I Am Being, I Am Life, and so on. God's name represents His person, so like God Himself, His name is also holy, just, and righteous. To be flippant with any of the revealed names of God found in Scripture is to disrespect, even deny the holiness of God Himself. Notice in the beginning of the Devil's "demonments" that he called himself "I AM ME," which is an example of taking the LORD's name in vain. He is taking something meant to indicate God and perverting it.

Before I was a Christian, and especially while I was in the military, my swearing and using the name of God in vain was constant. For a time after I was converted, I still took His name in vain, but then my conscience convicted me that it was wrong to do so. Though I had freedom to talk as I wished, I eventually stopped that swearing habit. I knew that since God was my heavenly Father, I should not speak as though He was nothing to me.

Demonment
FOUR

(YKW's fourth commandment: "Remember the Sabbath day, to keep it holy. Six days you shall labor and do all your work.")[1]

The fourth demonment: Work if you must, but whether you work or rest is meaningless to Me. Freedom of will and movement is what is important.

The Devil's Commentary

What does it matter? Do what suits you and what gains you an advantage in this dog-eat-dog world.

Some of my followers work non-stop, while others have stopped working. If working gets you what you want, work. How else are you going to get ahead of the pack? If you want to kick back, don't work. This having to "rest on the Sabbath" thing makes Me ill. Imagine, YKW dictating work habits when he's never had a paying job in his life.

Whether you work or not, make it count for Me. I will keep you busy – so much to do and so little time; so many to pre-

---

1   Some Christians consider the literal Sabbath, sundown on Friday to sundown on Saturday, to be the right time to worship God in community. Others, the vast majority, have from ancient times gathered for worship on Sunday, since there is evidence that the early Church did so. See John 20:19, Acts 20:7, 1 Cor. 16:2, and Revelation 1:10. Every day is a day of worship. Worshiping, assembling, or gathering on any particular day is a non-essential issue and not core to the Christian life.

vent from going over to the other side; so much confusion and division to create in YKW's workplace. The harvest is vast, and the laborers are many, but I need more and more laborers; I never have enough.

• •

A Christian's response

Work and rest – the great contrast. But the Devil, as usual, does not know or does not want others to know what the real issue is here.

In Genesis, God did His work of creation for six days, then He rested on the seventh. The fourth commandment springs directly from this pattern. God worked, then God rested; the precedent was established.[2]

Here, embedded in the work/rest contrast, is another dramatic historical prophecy. "Sabbath" in the Torah (the first five books of the Old Testament) means rest. Rest and work can be either physical or spiritual in nature. Physical work is one thing, but the concept of work is also used to describe the striving and struggling to achieve God's salvation.

It is commonly thought that a person must work, meaning be good, do good, be positive, don't hurt others, and so on, in order to earn salvation. In fact, no one can *earn* or work to gain salvation. "For by grace you have been saved through faith. And this is not your own doing; it is the gift of God, not a result of works, so that no one may boast."[3] Jesus is the one who worked; we rest in Him and what He did for us.

The writer of the New Testament book of Hebrews focuses on the difference between working, meaning keeping of the Law of Moses, and resting in Christ: "There remains a Sabbath rest for the people of God, for he who has entered God's rest will have also rested from his labor as God did from his."[4] The

---

2   Work and labor are honorable. God's intention is that we work, though according to Genesis 3:17-19, the work would not be easy. Work is a gift of God and can bring honor to him.

3   Ephesians 2:8-9.

4   See Hebrews 4:9-10

point is that Jesus has done the atoning work on the cross, taking sin upon Himself, thus satisfying the just demands of God. We can now enter into that rest by trusting in Jesus Christ as our Savior.

Two verses, one in Exodus and the other in the Gospel of Matthew, reveal that rest is a key concept God uses to reveal what salvation is really like:

In Exodus 33:14, God said, "My presence will go with you, and I [Yahweh] will give you rest."

In Matthew 11:28, Jesus said, "Come to me, all who labor and are heavy laden, and I will give you rest."

Jesus uses the word "labor" then adds the words exactly as in Exodus 33:14: "I will give you rest." This is no coincidence. God implanted in His Word (the Bible) the contrast between work and rest, which is prophecy at its best, to show us a picture of life in the Kingdom of God. The fourth commandment calls direct attention to the ultimate intention of God, that we rest eternally in the finished work of Jesus.

Demonment
FIVE

(YKW's fifth commandment: "Honor your father and your mother, that your days may be long in the land that the LORD your God is giving you.")

My fifth demonment: Your parents did not have you in mind - they were merely having sex. Do not honor parents for that lustful moment. Parents need not be honored unless it serves your purposes.

The Devil's Commentary

Face it – having babies is the way of the world, or else everything would come to an end. But YKW's fundamentalists get carried away about "obeying parents" and would have children blindly obey even their cruelest demands. My people use their common sense and reserve the right to rebel against undeserving parents, especially when dad or mom wants to put a damper on the fun. Parents care about you only if you achieve according to their impossibly high standards. Set your own standards and get away from theirs as soon as you can. Start living the life you want. You have better things to do than to kowtow to the people who dragged you into this miserable world.

Take my advice, children: Pit one parent against the other whenever it will profit you. That way you can give honor where honor is owed, to the parent who lets you have your own way, without wasting honor on the one who would keep you from fulfilling your destiny.

Take this advice also: Always watch out for number one. The old folks won't be around long anyway, but in the meantime they have a habit of wasting your time and money with their increasing illnesses. Let the state take care of them; that's why you pay taxes (at least those of you who haven't been smart enough to find a way out of it).

• •

A Christian's response

Parenting and family are central in God's plan for humanity, so He made us male and female and charged us to be fruitful and multiply.[1] Therefore, making love and making babies is not lustful but normal and natural. Parents and children need one another, and children need both parents to be involved in raising them. In this context the commandment puts male and female in parity. Both mother and father are owed equal honor.

The fifth commandment establishes the duties children have for their parents. God built a structure into the entire social fabric, based on honor and respect, without which there would be only chaos and the survival of the most powerful. Family obligations are the foundational forms of a safety net, created by God long before governmental entitlement programs.

The Hebrew word for "honor" means heavy or of great value. Children, at whatever age, should regard their parents as being of great value and consider their parents' needs, caring for them as they are able. Of course, not all parents do well with their children. Some parents commit terrible crimes against their children in ways that vividly reveal human depravity. A person abused by a parent will struggle with the fifth commandment, but it is better to make peace, even seeking reconciliation with such parents, than

---

1   See Genesis 1:26-28.

to continue to live burdened with hate and anger. This does not mean a hypocritical and shallow pretense of love but an understanding that they are still people made in God's image and therefore worthy of honor and care.

The commandment to "honor your father and mother" is basic to both the family and society. The social hierarchy that begins in one's family of origin is based on honor and respect. Civility and generosity starts with the child's devotion to his family members and extends to all levels of society and its government, from the local to the national. Any culture will fail, and its people will suffer greatly, when self-centered rebellion prevails. Without law and order, the law of the jungle prevails, which is just what Satan loves.

The Apostle Paul mentioned the fifth commandment in Ephesians 6:1-2: "Children, obey your parents in the Lord, for this is right. 'Honor your father and mother' (this is the first commandment with a promise)." Notice obedience (not submission) is owed to parents, and it must be "in the Lord." If a parent wants a child to do that which is *not* godly, then the child is *not* obligated to be obedient.

Paul also calls attention to a unique element in the commandment: the promise of a lengthy period of time in the land that God was giving the Hebrew people after the exodus from slavery in Egypt. It does not mean that people will live longer if they obey the commandment, but that they will possess the land a longer time by so doing. God knew that the honoring of parents would have a cascading effect in the life of the nation and would produce order and stability. Dishonoring parents jeopardizes the well-being of any society. This reality is abundantly evident in the histories of the nations on the earth.

Demonment
SIX

(YKW's sixth commandment: "You shall not murder.")

The sixth demonment: Do what is necessary to reach your highest potential and eliminate human roadblocks.

The Devil's Commentary

Never ignore this fact: "The strong survive." At your peril, dismiss a corollary to that: "Might makes right." If it means murder, so be it. Does this sound barbarous? It should not, because death is a fact of life, and everyone will die of something, sooner or later.

Many of the most renowned people in the world have been unafraid to exert dominance over others. The dregs of humanity are sponges, parasites, or suckers. The world is better off without these types draining precious resources that could be better utilized by my talented and ambitious disciples. The strong will eliminate obstacles to their own personal fulfillment.

Isn't that the underlying goal even in war? Don't we regularly reward the soldiers of this world who kill the greatest number of the enemy in the name of national honor? Those who are willing to do the dirty work will get to the finish line with the most medals. War is so much more gratifying than peace. It is the perfect platform for my kind of bravado and the perfect cover for eliminating the "undesirables."

My sentiments are nicely echoed in a myriad of films, television shows, and bestselling books about great killers and warriors, all glorifying violence and mayhem. This is where to find extreme excitement and the big money. Today's kids have the right idea: play violent video games until all squeamishness is eliminated about how to rid oneself of obstacles! So what if some of them act out their violent fantasies with mass school killings? The news shows need fodder for viewers who secretly wish they could be brave enough to plan and execute the same escapades.

Guns, bombs, and all death machines, blood spilled, bodies torn – glorious! I am unapologetic about this. I am a professional hitman of the highest caliber.

• •

A Christian's response

People are made in the image of God; therefore, murder is a direct affront to God. This is why, from his first appearance in the Garden of Eden, Satan made sure Adam and Eve would experience death as the separation from God. When he lacks the ability to divert sinners from repenting and receiving forgiveness and salvation, Satan resorts to lies and homicide.

In his desperate rebellion against God, the Devil will do anything to prevent someone from becoming a born-again child of God the Father, and will not blink at murder, because a dead person is then beyond saving, and with one victim out of the way, he moves on to target the next. The Devil does not usually murder directly. He uses his disciples to do his dirty work for him, all the while pushing the idea that it takes great strength and bravery to pull the trigger.

Murder does not advance the cause of the murderer, except perhaps temporarily. Most often, murderers are themselves murdered by those seeking revenge or by a government that objects to the wanton abuse of its citizens. Murderers go to prison, and for long periods; some are never released. If they are not incarcerated physically they may be locked in the darkness of their own conscience. Stealing another person's life will weigh heavily on the mind of all but those with a severely seared conscience. Murder is a death sentence for all concerned. The victims line up on both sides of the weapon.

The Hebrew word for "murder" is used forty-seven times in the Old Testament and means the deliberate, unlawful killing of a human being. It is not used for the killing of animals, killing in war, capital punishment, or self-defense. An individual, acting on his or her own, is prohibited from deliberately killing another human being. This is murder. A society cannot abide such contempt for human life.

In regard to war, Christians differ on this point but usually justify human killing in a so-called "just" war or when one nation invades another unprovoked for political or economic gain. In the case of capital punishment, again Christians are divided, but as far as Scripture goes, in the context of the Old Testament, when a nation executes those who commit capital crimes it is not considered "murder" of the perpetrator but just punishment. It is generally understood that the sixth commandment cannot be used to support pacifism or the abolishment of capital punishment. These must be argued on other grounds. The New Testament writers do not weigh in on the issues of what is and what is not murder, except that Jesus implies that being angry with someone is tantamount to mentally murdering him, a precursor to actual murder.[1]

One would think it poor public relations for the Devil to admit he is a murderer. However, the Devil cannot help it. Murder is at his core, and that fact will never change. Jesus said about him, "He was a murderer from the beginning and has nothing to do with the truth, because there is no truth in him".[2]

---

1   See Matthew 5:21-22.
2   John 8:44b

Demonment
SEVEN

(YKW's seventh commandment: "You shall not commit adultery.")

***T**he seventh demonment: Freely indulge yourselves and let your hormones guide you. Be fruitful and multiply!*

The Devil's Commentary

YKW is sexually repressed and foists that malady on his followers. This law is just another expression of prejudice against people expressing their normal sexuality, which is built into the genes, hardwired into the brain, and driven by some of the most powerful drugs there are: hormones. YKW can't have it both ways. If he made humans sexually alive, then he's fooling himself to think he can suppress the very thing that makes them feel good. We're talking about mutual consent here. The moralists just can't understand the essential truth that there is really nothing unnatural or bad when it comes to sex; there are merely the perverted attitudes and opinions of those who think that YKW's bible is the revealed truth. This is one of the reasons I have taken up the work of writing my own bible, so that the truth might be known.

And adultery, what does that mean? In biblical times, only the woman was forbidden to copulate with someone other than her husband. The man could do what he pleased, as long as he was willing to take the other woman into his home as a second (or third or?) wife. I say, if a weak man can't keep control of his own wife, he deserves to lose the loose woman to the better man. Since I am always the better man, I have all I want. Be like Me and you will have all you want, too. How else are the strong to "be fruitful and multiply"?

• •

A Christian's response

With the introduction of sin into the human equation, the drive for procreation became perverted and the sexual appetite was exaggerated; the natural and normal balance was lost. The effort to fulfill the sexual drive turned many to both obsessive/compulsive behavior and disregard of the marriage pledge.

The prohibition against adultery implies the stealing of another's private and intimate experience of love. What should have been the exclusive privilege of two people is torn apart and violated.

Adultery and all the other perversions of sexuality are common in the world at large, extending back to ancient times. When the seventh commandment was given, some thirteen to fifteen hundred years before the days of Jesus' earthly ministry, pagan sexual practices were commonly accepted, everything from incest to homosexuality, sex with children, sex with animals, and temple prostitution. Much of that was connected to the cult worship of pagan gods. Yahweh God wanted the Hebrew people to be different – thus the seventh commandment.[1]

The prohibition against adultery fits in with the overall biblical view of human sexuality. Sexual pleasure is part of love and an opportunity to give and receive intimate expressions of love. It was intended for far more than procreation to assure that the human race continues.

---

1   The Law of Moses expanded on the seventh commandment in Exodus 22:16 and Leviticus 18:6-23.

The Song of Solomon reveals the potential depth of love between a man and a woman. Healthy human beings can enjoy sex all their lives. Some say it even gets better as the years go by.

Human sexuality is only one aspect of human love, which goes much deeper than physical pleasure. A relationship based solely on sex will be a poor one and is not likely to continue to satisfy. Sex is complicated and baffling, and multitudes of fears and obsessions surround it. Few people are able to analyze themselves about it openly and honestly, and wrong uses of sex usually thwart that possibility altogether.

A question: When is sex the best? Here is my opinion. Sex is best between a married man and woman who care for and want to please each other. Over the course of years, the best sex is discovered and practiced freely and without guilt or fear. Christians, long married, discover levels of intimacy and pleasure most people never achieve. Good sex, set in the context of a committed marriage relationship, is slowly developed; it does not come quickly. And married people don't need to be in a hurry about it; they have a lifetime to learn what sex is all about. Some Christians I know are super sexy and are loving every minute of it. While that may sound odd to many, following the Creator's ways is far better than messing up our lives with stolen or perverted sexuality. The biblical model gives the best chance for love and depth in the sexual union.

Demonment
EIGHT

(YKW's eighth commandment: "You shall not steal")

The eighth demonment: If you need it take it, and besides, everyone is corrupt. To steal is only natural.

The Devil's Commentary

What some call "stealing" is really just how the downtrodden use their talents to survive in a miserable world. They are actually heroes, liberating what should rightfully be theirs from those who have more than they need. Will the rich give the poor what they need? No they will not. The rich are hoarders and they made their wealth off the backs of the oppressed. What will the poor do? Take what they can get is the answer, and it is perfectly justified.

If you are strong and privileged and have plenty already, then I say make sure the filthy looters don't break in and take what you worked so hard (or didn't) to obtain.

There are many creative modern ways to express one's thievery: The boss won't notice a few office supplies missing once in a while. Besides, all companies have "inventory slippage" built into the bottom line. What do they buy insurance for, if they think nothing is going to go missing? That little jumper cable you put on your electrical meter to cut out the utility company shows how industrious you are. The library books you don't return won't be missed for months. The wallet you "found" in someone's pocket is itching to be lifted and put to better use. The fruit you "sampled" in the grocery store should have been put out for customers' benefit. The taxes you creatively "avoided" paying would only have paid for pork barrel projects in someone else's district. That unprotected "identity" that some idiot left lying around the internet is begging to be given to someone more deserving. The village you just overran in wartime expects to be pillaged; that's just one of the rules of the game.

You get the picture. Everyone "liberates" stuff to some extent, and to call it stealing is both an exaggeration and an over-simplification. It really wastes my time to argue about minute definitions. Ignore YKW's eighth commandment; it is hopelessly out of date and oppressive.

I am most committed to my own kind of liberating, which is to snatch a poor lost soul from ending up in the clutches of YKW. I will entice, deceive, lie, whatever works, because YKW never earned or deserved anyone's loyalty. They owe their devotion to Me! I give them all the goodies they could ever hope to steal. I am the true expression of their deepest desires!

• •

A Christian's response

To steal means to take for oneself what belongs to another.[1] In a technologically advanced society stealing may occur in many forms, for example, the electronic theft of data and intellectual material including identity theft, as well as unreported income, insider trading, lying to get a loan, and the list goes on. Imagine the extent of stealing that goes on in governments around the world. Some societies are reduced to third-world economic status by extreme levels of corruption. Stealing may be the most widespread of all forms of wrongdoing.

It has been said that all the ten commandments have to

---

1   Stealing may include kidnapping, as in Genesis 40:15.

do with stealing. One, to have other gods is to steal from God the worship owed to Him alone. Two, to make an idol, either out of stone or wood, or something mental or emotional, and worship that as a god is again stealing the worship that is rightfully the Creator's only. Three, using God's name inappropriately is to steal the respect and honor due Him. Four, to use the Sabbath entirely for your own pleasure is to steal from God worship due Him. Five, to not honor your father and mother is to steal what is owed to them. Six, to murder is to steal a life away. Seven, to commit adultery is to steal love and affection due a spouse. Eight, our present commandment which makes the direct statement: "You shall not steal." Nine, to swear falsely, which is lying and deceipt, is to steal justice from a neighbor. Ten, to have unwarranted desire for what belongs to a neighbor is to set the stage for direct thievery and adultery. Stealing is all-encompassing.

The Devil's false notion of entitlement is a wicked concept used for justifying all his actions, starting from the first time he tried to steal the sovereignty of God in the Garden of Eden. Satan encourages us to think that if another has what we need then we are permitted to steal it. In some sub-cultures it is systemic and inbred. The thief sees victims as suckers who deserve to be exploited. Stealing may be fueled by anger at not having what others have, a sense of entitlement, or a feeling of being victimized and therefore justified in getting retribution. There are many motivations driving a thief, but whatever they might be, however excused the thief might think he or she is, the God who gives us all things says, "Do not steal."

Demonment NINE

(YKW's ninth commandment: "You shall not bear false witness against your neighbor.")

*T*he ninth demonment: Do not be concerned about what others think of you, including your neighbors. Say whatever you must to advance your own agenda.

The Devil's Commentary

Being nice to a neighbor is fine if that works for you. If they are believers in YKW you may be able to compromise them in some way and tarnish their reputation, which would advance my kingdom. Work on pointing out the contradictions in that book of theirs. Hold them to an impossibly high standard (which you do not intend to maintain yourself), and remind them often about their failures. Scour the newspapers and the internet to find stories about how some pastor or churchgoer has been caught doing something scandalous. Then find ways to make his failures known publicly; for example, contact newspapers, stick a sign on his lawn, start an email and social media campaign, and most assuredly maintain lively gossip. What fun to see them so harassed!

Gossip is a wonderful tool. Spreading scandalous stories around is almost magical; it doesn't matter if there is any truth to the tales. People love to believe bad things about others; in fact, it becomes addictive for some. You can at least isolate neighbors from YKW's people and prevent them from having any influence. I love rumors.

And if you find yourself in a court of law, just pretend you mean it when they ask you to swear by "almighty YKW" but say whatever you have to, if it saves your own neck or makes you look like an upstanding citizen. Forget any so-called damage it could do to anyone else. Always look out for number one. The principle is: work to set one against another. I love division and rivalry.

• •

A Christian's response

The ninth commandment has a judicial element to it. Justice depends on truthfulness, and without that, social systems break down. Accountability in a court is required for fairness to prevail.

Among neighbors, friends, family members, businesspersons, and citizens, honesty is essential. Without truthfulness, trust dissolves and relationships fall apart.

Let's look at the word "neighbor." Jesus told a story usually referred to as the "Parable of the Good Samaritan," in which He defined who is really a neighbor.[1] The historical context is important. Terrible hostility existed between the Jews and the Samaritans. The Samaritans were descended from intermarriage between Jews and Assyrians. The enmity was so bad that the two groups avoided all contact with each other, and talking together was taboo.

In the story, a Jewish man is robbed and left for dead on the road. Two high-status Jewish "religious people" observe the wounded man but do nothing. Then a Samaritan comes upon the incapacitated man and takes care of him with considerable expenditure of time and money. He even takes him to an inn and pays for his medical care, room, and board. Jesus then asks His listeners, "Which of these three, do you think, proved to be a neighbor to the man who fell among

---

1   See Luke 10:25-37.

the robbers?"[2]

The answer is plain. The Samaritan, the hated Samaritan, proved to be the Jewish man's neighbor. Jesus greatly broadened the definition of who must be considered a neighbor, an issue that was hotly contested among the religious leaders of that day. "Neighbor" is not restricted to someone who lives near us, nor to someone who is a member of our clan, tribe, religion, or nation. Our neighbor is whoever needs help and friendship, which is just about everyone, to one degree or another. It is not a stretch to conclude that *everyone* may become a neighbor.

We should be truthful with our neighbors and not scandalize or mistreat them. We should be ready to give them as much aid as we can. We should not give empty promises (which is the basic meaning of the Hebrew word translated "false"), but as best we can, do what we say we will do and be who we say we will be.

---

2   Luke 10:36.

Demonment
TEN

(YKW's tenth commandment: "You shall not covet your neighbor's house; you shall not covet your neighbor's wife, or his male servant, or his female servant, or his ox, or his donkey, or anything that is your neighbor's.")

The tenth demonment: You are free to appreciate what others have and be ambitious, even cunning, about obtaining it. I make no law that thwarts freedom of thought, which cannot be enforced anyway.

The Devil's Commentary

"Covet" – what a stupid word. No one even knows what it means. The truth is that YKW makes declarations that are simply intended to confuse and intimidate. He's even trying to regulate your *thoughts*, not just something you act on! Let go of the fear of breaking these oppressive, guilt-producing commandments, which are only devices used by religionists to prevent us from exploring life's possibilities.

If you desire something, go after it. Of course, be careful and do not land in jail. What matters is doing and getting what you want. Life is short and full of trouble, so who cares anyway? When you're dead, you're dead, and that is all there is. You know you can trust Me on that one.

. . . .
A Christian's response

The last of the Ten Commandments seems to follow closely with the ninth commandment, as the word "neighbor" is again present. It may be that the tenth commandment amplifies the ninth. But there is more to it than that.

God's Ten Commandments conclude with what may be considered a summary of the whole and goes to the heart of the human condition: the trouble all starts within our hearts and minds. We want what we do not have, so we take action to get what we want. First we reject the honor and worship of God, then we create idols of material things. We refuse to rest in the provision of God, we let our physical desires go unrestrained, we lie, cheat, steal, and kill to satisfy ourselves. In short, it all starts with coveting others and what belongs to them.

Covet means having an undue, selfish desire for something that is not yours. James, the half-brother of Jesus, explains it this way:

> What causes quarrels and what causes fights among you? Is it not this, that your passions are at war within you? You desire and do not have, so you murder. You covet and cannot obtain, so you fight and quarrel (James 4:1-2a).

Regarding covetousness, John warned in his letter,

> Do not love the world or the things in the world. If anyone loves the world, the love of the Father is not in him. For all that is in the world – the desires of the flesh and the desires of the eyes and pride in possessions – is not from the Father but is from the world. And the world is passing away along with its desires,

but whoever does the will of God abides forever (1 John 2:15-17).

God knows us well, and that is why He has given us His commandments. They are meant for our good and not for the purpose of preventing us from having pleasure or "exploring life's possibilities."

One last word: Jesus, as recorded in John's Gospel, said that the thief, or Satan, "comes only to steal and kill and destroy." That is an incredibly accurate description of the Devil's agenda. Then Jesus added, "I came that they may have life and have it abundantly."[1]

---

1   John 10:10a and b.

The
BeBaditudes

Editor's note: A beatitude denotes blessing or being blessed. A Blessing denotes happiness, well-being, or joy. The original list of beatitudes is found in Matthew 5:1-12:

> Seeing the crowds, [Jesus] went up on the mountain, and when he sat down, his disciples came to him. [2] And he opened his mouth and taught them, saying: [3] "Blessed are the poor in spirit, for theirs is the kingdom of heaven. [4] "Blessed are those who mourn, for they shall be comforted. [5] "Blessed are the meek, for they shall inherit the earth. [6] "Blessed are those who hunger and thirst for righteousness, for they shall be satisfied. [7] "Blessed are the merciful, for they shall receive mercy. [8] "Blessed are the pure in heart, for they shall see God. [9] "Blessed are the peacemakers, for they shall be called sons of God. [10] "Blessed are those who are persecuted for righteousness' sake, for theirs is the kingdom of heaven. [11] "Blessed are you when others revile you and persecute you and utter all kinds of evil against you falsely on my account. [12] Rejoice and be glad, for your reward is great in heaven, for so they persecuted the prophets who were before you.

The Devil shows his true colors in his "Bebaditudes." By now the reader does not need a Christian's Response in order to see the Devil's underlying intentions. The Devil starts his entries...

The first Bebaditude: Happy are the proud, the rich, and the self-confident, those who know what they want and get it.

Avoid the poor; they are not worthy of your attention. Suggest to them that they need to curse YKW and die. (Job's wife had it right.[1])

The poor have only themselves to blame, whether poor in spirit or just plain poor. They brought it all upon themselves; they are nothing more than losers, so let them rot. If you can't survive and succeed, then you are worthless and should not be consuming valuable resources.

YKW and company waste so much energy helping the poor, and of course they are proud of themselves for doing it. They do so thinking they must "help" others in order to get angel wings, halos, and a harp.

However, I see things from a better perspective: I welcome the poor, the depressed, the discouraged, the losers of the world; in fact, I delight in their being just like they are. They are unlovable, miserable, and dirty. They die young and come to my place without Me having to trouble myself much, though it sometimes amazes Me which ones and how many of them my enemy snatches away from Me. I can always count on winning plenty of the rich, the self-satisfied, the proud, the powerful. I get more than you might imagine. But sometimes the poor start looking for hope and then run across an emissary of the enemy, hearing what I don't want them to hear. My adversary actually seeks these people out. It has been this way from the very beginning. It is sickening.

---

1   He must mean Job 2:9.

*T**he second Bebaditude: Gratified are those who know** they are happy when they pursue what they want with* *abandon or determination without regard to the needs or rights of others.*

Convince those who mourn that they deserve their sorrowing and sadness, because they are bad people and YKW hates them. My disciples rush into life, savoring each moment, and refuse to waste their time being overly concerned with bad feelings other people might have. Follow your bliss!

Life is getting and retaining power and the wealth that secures it. The good life is filled with things to enjoy, such as food, drink, sex, and more sex. Comfort lies in not having to rely on anyone or anything else to feel on top of the world.

Don't worry when things do go awry, because I will lead you to the next opportunity to fulfill your desires. Feed your lust and you will be comforted. That "repentance" nonsense is just that. Apologize and sympathize if it is to your advantage. Always keep an eye on what you can get out of any situation.

*T**he third Bebaditude: Contented are those who trust in** Me, for they will not be meek, and they will not grovel* *before anyone; rather they will make others cringe before them and will gain the kingdoms of this world.*

The meek are weak and will inherit nothing, as logic clearly shows. These lost souls are vulnerable, so take advantage of them any way you can. The strong survive and prosper. Is this not the dominant worldview and something plainly observed in nature? Is this not the way YKW made things in the first place? Survival of the fittest!

Those who follow Me are rebels at heart. I AM ME, the Chief Rebel in the universe and their archetypical representative, alone should be worshiped. I am the Chief Anarchist;

I am against all that has to do with YKW. I counter the good with the bad; the beautiful with the ugly. I revel in destroying the little that the cowards and weaklings cling to. I do it with clever deception, hate, and murder. Be as I am, do as I do, and you will satisfy the rage that burns within you. In the end you will have earned the right to be with I AM ME, your King, forever.

The fourth Bebaditude: Glad are those who seek after what I offer, the pride of self and possessions and the desires of the flesh and the eyes. Hunger and thirst for these and you will be satiated.

Seek and you will find all that your twisted little heart desires. "Twisted" is a spin on "sinful," and sinful we will be, since this is what your hearts and minds are wired for. We are honest enough to admit that what we hunger for is sinful in the eyes of YKW. Never mind the consequences; no one really believes in an "eternity in heaven" with the prudish and boring saints. Set your goals on what can be grasped now. You do not have to look very deeply into yourself to know the real motives that call out to you.

The only "righteousness" worth hungering after is self-righteousness. Don't let the do-gooders try to tell you to follow some impossibly high standards that YKW set out in his book. That book is full of contradictions anyway. Determine your own spirituality and excel in it. Avoid looking too deeply into yourself, for you want to maintain the strongest possible sense of self-righteousness.

The fifth Bebaditude: Delighted are those who know that it is no advantage to show mercy to anyone unless it helps you get what you want, including rewards here and now.

Show no mercy – this is our code!

"Mercy" is what YKW and his meager little band practice.

They do it with such obviously mixed motives; it is laughable that they get any reward at all. But my followers do not show mercy; it is not natural in this jungle of a world. Hit them when they're down, and they won't get back up to bother you again.

Those who fall into trouble deserve it; it is their destiny to suffer. We believe in karma, what goes around comes around. Those who are working out the mess they made of their past lives have to fix it themselves without mercy from us or anyone else. We will not interfere with someone who is working out natural karmic consequences.

Those who follow in my way are strong and do not need mercy. Think about it. What is it that you need that I cannot provide? Now, if you are tempted to believe that there is a judgment ahead, which is merely a YKW scare tactic, then the worst-case scenario would be that you would be with Me and my angels.   talking big party now, and for a whole long time. It doesn't get any better than that!

The sixth Bebaditude: Rewarded are those who follow Me with all their heart, for they shall see Me and know Me as I AM ME.

The pure are those who do my will and have not polluted themselves by contact with YKW. Those who do my bidding will abide with Me forever. The great reward is to see Me in all my glory. Am I not Lucifer, the Day Star, the Son of Dawn?[2] Did not even Moses describe Me as "crafty?"[3]

Adam and Eve became my disciples and did my bidding. They did as I suggested so they could leave that boring Garden of Eden, which spared them from having to be with YKW all the time. Then they experienced real life rather than having everything handed to them on a platter. They learned the difference between good and evil; they became mature;

---

2   See Isaiah 14:12.
3   See Genesis 3:1.

they beheld the glories of evil.

Follow the example of Adam and Eve: disobey, ignore, and reject the commandments of YKW. Be impure of heart. The so-called "pure in heart" know nothing and experience nothing but are trapped in YKW's little world – forever, I remind you. But to see and know I AM ME is the greatest high that life has to offer.

The seventh Bebaditude: Satisfied are those who create division and factions, who stir up trouble in families, clans, tribes, and nations. These are truly my warriors.

War and death are the glories we live for. Life is a battle, the strong succeed, and the weak are destroyed. My followers are true warriors.

It is not in our interest to have peaceful relations, either in the macro or micro states. Make division among members of families, neighbors, friends, and particularly in your churches, so you will see who is really on your side. Take it to the highest levels so that wars will abound, for it is in war that the mighty dominate and thrive.

"Reconciliation," "forgiveness," and "restoration" are repugnant words, used by the weak and the meek, because they have no other hope than to get everyone to "make nice." Those who seek and promote these notions should be punished and discarded, by shunning or by murder. When you reject them and their vile notions, then you will be called the sons and daughters of Lucifer.

The eighth Bebaditude: Pleased are the persecutors of those who belong to YKW, for their reward will be great in my kingdom.

Curse those who stand up for YKW – ridicule them, belittle them, and persecute them. You will discover allies that you never thought possible. Many who appear to follow YKW are simply doing so out of a sense of tradition or cultural identity and do not really belong to YKW. When times of persecution come, many of the "faithful" show their true colors.

In dark or primitive regions, my people beat, kill, burn, rape, rob, and throw into prison those who dare to publicly proclaim belief in YKW. In more advanced societies, I employ the more nuanced approaches, including humiliations, intellectual demeaning, strategically-placed college professors, financial and sexual scandalizing, and other rather sophisticated tactics. Many of YKW's people are immature, weak, and easily deceived. Just when they think they are looking so good, it is great fun to embarrass them in the newspapers, on television news shows, and all over the internet.

My public relations specialists are working non-stop to make the followers of YKW look foolish, behind the times, and at odds with science and modern paradigms. One of my favorite tactics is to get YKW's sponsors distracted into social and political agendas rather than more dangerous activities like preaching and missions.

It definitely looks as though I am winning; my kingdom is coming. You know that I am speaking the absolute truth and would never lie to my devoted and beloved followers. Someday soon, we will all be together.

Final Instructions for the Devil's Angels

I warn you to remember that the essential strategy we employ is convincing people that they are good enough and do not need saving. Remember how the "bad" people – tax collectors, prostitutes, lepers, sinners – flocked to J…s. Okay, they knew they needed rescuing, but most people are not imitations of Stalin and Hitler. Most just plod along, doing all the usual sinning – sex games, stealing here and there, telling little lies – you know, the regular stuff. These people will do some good things, too, so take advantage of such behavior and convince them they are good enough, probably racking up more good than bad points.

Waffle on that good and bad bit. Most days, on the news or in the newspapers, there are stories of people robbing, raping, and pillaging. Remind our disciples of all the good they do: volunteering, helping out the poor at Thanksgiving and Christmas, giving at the office, recycling, and a host of other worthwhile endeavors. Convince them they are not like the really bad people, and if there is a "God," he is probably taking notes. Encourage them to be good citizens. Yes, it is a contradiction I make: help people be good yet corrupt them to ruin if you can. But I tell you, statistically we do better by encouraging people to be good and to rely more upon their own goodness than anything else we do.

Abandon efforts to convince people they are good enough, whenever you can instead convince them they are too bad to ever get YKW's pardon.

Never cease from reminding those who even begin to consider becoming one of YKW's people that the "saints" are all hypocrites repressed by guilt. Offer them freedom from inane rules and stupid reliance on looking perfect.

The preaching of what the enemy calls the "gospel" must be stopped. If that "gospel" is presented, even though somewhat poorly, then we are in trouble, because YKW's Spirit begins to work on the listeners. When that happens, we lose. Our strategy goes for naught, or often does, when such a circumstance occurs. If necessary, stick your fingers in a person's ears. You would be surprised how effective that is.

Tempt preachers to change their focus. Get them to talk about politics, local or national. Any cause will do.

One way to stick it to "gospel" preachers is to incite church-goers to criticize them by pointing out how unloving it is to talk about sin and hell.

Bring troublesome feuds into the home. Division is fertile ground for accomplishing our aims.

Envy is a powerful motivator. Make a preacher financially successful for doing things that do not really threaten us. Then he is both a target of the enviers and he is helping our cause.

Get people excited about churchy spiritual activities like healing, or miracles, or lengthening legs, or seeing the glittering powdery substance in the air that they call "angel dust" (not to be confused with one of the many street drugs I love to promote) – you know, the usual bag of tricks that will get their attention away from YKW's essential message.

O nce we get people jazzed on the trance and meditation aspects of their religions, we can get them to completely empty their minds and leave the door open. Then we get to slip in unnoticed.

D istract from YKW's core message by inviting people to think that his religion is all about how they feel. You feel good, you are blessed. You feel bad, you must be cursed.

These are fine for starters.

Epilogue from the Christian Commentator

The Devil's words are appealing and enticing; they speak to the arrogant pride we humans have embedded in us. The Devil's bible invites free rein to the body's desires kept deep in our hearts. The end of it all is an eternity spent in hell.

This is no game! The Devil is a murderer from the beginning, a fact we now know well. Eternal death awaits those who follow that liar, and it is a death of ultimate horror.

Death is of two kinds: *bios* is biological death and *zoe* is spiritual death. All will die biologically, but all will be raised from that biological death and have spiritual life that will be lived out either in heaven or in hell. The Devil's disciples have no idea how supremely horrific that will be. From the Devil's bible, we can now understand to some degree the depth of the Devil's hatred for those made in the image of our Creator God.

Now, please accept one last word from me, an ordinary Christian who loves God's Bible from cover to cover and the Savior whose story it tells. I must repeat how Jesus put it: "The thief comes only to steal and kill and destroy. I came that they may have life and have it abundantly" (John 10:10).

Other Books by Kent Philpott

*Awakenings in America and
the Jesus People Movement*

How Christinas Cast Out Demons Today

*Are You Really Born Again?
Understanding True and False Conversion*

Are You Being Duped?

Why I Am a Christian

For Pastors of Small Churches

How to Care for Your Pastor

EVP

Available at www.evpbooks.com

CPSIA information can be obtained at www.ICGtesting.com
Printed in the USA
LVOW12s0438240713

344271LV00002B/2/P